PROMISE

A Story of Race, Culture and Black
Potential

Ron Tinsley

Adamsterdam House

Preface

Once in a generation a book comes along that offers all the solutions for young people, old people and everyone in between. A book that, after reading you walk away feeling like everything is all right in the world.

If you're looking for a book like that-put this book down and walk away.

This book hopes to address issues under-privileged and minority youth face in the United States and the overarching effects those issues have on these kids. The story is told through the eyes and adventures of me as a young man growing up in an era spanning the Jim Crow era to present day. It encompasses my circuitous journey to overcome the psychological barriers that were imposed on me and that I in turn imposed upon myself.

This book is for the young minority men and women who, if nurtured, can become part of the solution, and if not, could become the problem. It's a call-out to America to recognize the cost of ignoring the promise of these young people as well as the incredible potential of bringing them into the fold.

I am not a writer. I don't have a degree in journalism, Black history or even American history, for that matter. I do however feel the need to write this book, partly as a testament to my life as a Black American who followed a less-than-traditional route to achieve my successes. I also am writing this book as a way to encourage and inspire the promising Black and Brown children who if given the chance, will no doubt rise up and achieve far greater successes than I have, despite the encumbrances imposed upon them.

Also, just to clarify, I am not a spokesperson for Black Americans, nor is Al Sharpton, Jesse Jackson, or any other Black American. We are as diverse a group of people as the whole human race, and to take the characteristics of a few of us and assume they apply to all of us is like saying all trees are oak trees or all fish are tuna.

Ron Tinsley ~ 2023

Dedication

I ARRIVED IN LAHAINA, Maui in the summer of 1973 and it became home.

I instantly fell in love with old Lahaina; the Pioneer Inn where you could feel the spirits of generations of seafarers coming to port after time at sea, the majestic banyan tree that was old even then, the Maui Bell, the local dive—every town needs one, the Lahaina Broiler where the little black crabs would scramble for scraps at your toes as you dined, the sea wall where we would pause and absorb the legendary Maui sunsets which will always be a part of me. And most of all, the people of Lahaina and the aloha spirit that resides in all who have ever lived there.

This book is dedicated to the remembrance of those who perished during the devastating fire of 2023, the many who were left homeless, and those who have lost loved ones. This book is also dedicated to those of us experiencing the heartache of losing something of such beauty that can never be replaced.

May the aloha spirit live on in the aina of old Lahaina and the ohana of those who have lived there.

Aloha and mahalo nui loa to old Lahaina.

Identifiers:

Library of Congress Control Number: 2023914731

LCCN – Print: 2023914731

ISBN: 979-8-218-95900-5 (print)

ISBN: 979-8-218-95901-2 (ebook)

Publisher: Adamsterdam House

Edited by David Aretha, with comments and suggestions by countless others.

First edition 2023

Chapter 1

CINCINNATI, 1963

I T HAD STARTED OVER something trivial in a dark dead-end street in the downtown slums, a part of Cincy that had once been some mayor's idea of urban development, but that over the years had descended into a series of narrow cobblestone alleys kept in a constant state of darkness by the towering, dirty brick buildings shadowing them.

I was hanging with my friend R.D.—a whip of a guy who gave the impression of a coiled spring ready to let loose. He had one distinguishing characteristic that made him stand out: he wasn't afraid of anyone or anything. We were two young teenagers always out exploring different neighborhoods. On this day we were in a neighborhood we had no business in; we had a habit of doing that. A dangerous thing to do in this part of Cincy, but if you weren't willing to take some chances, you just stayed home.

We were walking past a narrow passageway when we heard a commotion: shouts and sounds of scuffling, underscored by loud music being played. Curiosity got the best of us, and we ventured down a narrow alley that opened into a courtyard, surrounded by tall, dark windows. Debris spilling from overturned trash cans exuded a fetid odor of weeks-old, uncollected, rotting garbage. It was a blistering hot Midwest summer day, the heat so stifling that it sucked the moisture from every pore. Windows were open, curtains billowing and folks hanging out of the windows, watching the scene below like a sporting event. Stevie Wonder's "Fingertips" blasted from one side of the courtyard, the Miracles' "Mickey's Monkey" from the other as a counterpoint. What we saw was a too-common scene in the projects. Two dudes were squaring off in the middle of the street, surrounded by a crowd of people egging them on.

"Come on, kick his ass, man. He ain't no good. You can take that motherfucker."

It was obvious from the attitude of the onlookers that one of the fighters was local, and one wasn't. Judging from their moves, I could tell they were two equally badass bangers who could have, and probably did, rule in most situations.

One of them was a tall, sinewy guy, handsome, with sharp features and a "do," the straightened hairstyle that was popular at the time. He had scars around his eyes and one on his upper lip that told me he was battle-tested, but he still managed to retain his good looks—a pretty boy.

The other fighter had the type of body that indicated he'd spent time in the "Big House": prison tatts and muscles bulging in places where they shouldn't have been, like he had had a lot of time on his hands recently. Nothing good-looking about him; he had a protruding brow, long arms for his size—kinda caveman-looking—and dead eyes that told me he was ugly inside and out, like he was mad at his mother, and the world, for being born so ugly.

Pretty Boy danced and jabbed, bobbed and weaved, like Sugar Ray. He was obviously a good fighter, but more importantly, he looked good—which was crucial 'cause that's how you got your reputation in the projects. Kicking ass was one thing, but if you did it with style, that moved you into a completely different category.

Muscle Man, on the other hand, was all business. The look in his eyes scared me, and I wasn't even involved. He moved in flat-footed, shuffling steps, like he was walking something down, like a panther methodically stalking his prey, intent on one thing and one thing only.

They went back and forth exchanging blows, grappling, hitting the ground, rolling around, back up, back and forth. It was a pretty even fight, but little by little, you could see Muscle Man was getting the upper hand.

Pretty Boy was running out of steam. His do looked more like do-do, hair sticking up all over his head, sweat pouring down his face. He didn't dance as much anymore, and he was staggering, sucking air, trying to figure out how to get the best of this big ugly hulk in front of him. He had hit Muscle Man with everything he had, but he just kept coming—like a bad case of acne.

Then I realized the taunting and shit-talking had stopped, as if people realized this wasn't just another short bout where somebody tapped out and walked away. This was something more serious, these guys had some bad blood between them that was going to be settled that day.

Moving in close, grappling, each trying to get an advantage; Muscle Man managed to get Pretty Boy in a chokehold and held on like a pit bull, exerting pressure through his oversize arms like a vice, digging deeper, putting everything into it.

Pretty Boy struggled to get out of it. Twisting, turning, throwing elbows, trying to break free, all to no avail. After a while his struggles grew weaker. He was running out of energy...and out of breath. He began to lose coordination; his arms became wet noodles.

Then the struggling stopped.

I've seen lots of fights in my life, but I will always remember the look in Pretty Boy's eyes. A bleak look, like prey in the jaws of a predator. In it was the moment of realization that he wasn't going to make it out of this one.

Muscle Man had won the fight, but it was obvious that his intention didn't end there—he had something more final in mind.

He looked over at one of his boys and said, "Let me know when this nigga's dead."

Finally, one of them nodded; the killer held on for a while longer—then let go.

Pretty Boy fell like a tree. Nothing in his body was able to stop his fall because nothing worked anymore.

When his head hit the ground, it made a loud "THUNK," a hollow popping sound like when you plunk a ripe watermelon. I looked at him lying there and realized he had pissed his pants and wasn't breathing. It wasn't anything like what you see in the movies; not glamorous, not at all pretty.

A reverence fell over the crowd—like a funeral. Curtains were drawn, windows closed, and people started drifting away.

Then R.D. tapped me on the shoulder and said, "Hey, man, let's get out of here before the cops get here."

We walked away because we knew that was when the real ass-kicking would start, and they wouldn't stop with just the remaining bad motherfucker. We didn't want to be collateral damage.

It didn't bother me at the time because I was a different person than I am now. I had seen people die before, and fights were just a part of our neighborhood. But now I sometimes have dreams of the haunted look in Pretty Boy's eyes and wonder if I could have, should have done something. Probably not because I would've ended up getting my ass kicked. I was out of my neighborhood, outnumbered, and fourteen years old—still a kid.

Calling the cops was out of the question; you just didn't. Cops always came in full force and didn't bother trying to decipher who the innocent bystanders were. They assumed if you were in the area, you were involved, which gave them the right to kick your ass. The Protect and Serve part of their motto somehow didn't apply to us.

There was not much we could do about the cops. They'd stop us, slam us up against a car, and rough us up just for being Black in our own neighborhood. We were powerless. In fact, if you resisted or even gave them a dirty look, you stood a chance of getting the life choked out of you. At worst, you might be shot; at best, just beaten up. If it was their word against ours, it was always their word that was taken as truth, so out of our frustration we turned against each other. We fought each other; our dogs fought each other; we stabbed, shot, and killed each other—the second of two wrongs that would never make a right.

There was one cop, Joe Beatty—an oversized, muscular cop who used his billy-club like he enjoyed it. If you looked at him wrong, he'd jam his club so deep in your gut you'd be shitting splinters. If you saw him coming, the best thing you could do was disappear, but he had a way of suddenly appearing out of nowhere, and when he caught you, it was one of those "aw shit" moments. Didn't matter if you were doing something wrong or not. If you were on the street, he assumed you were up to no good, so he felt justified in taking you down.

This was the '60s in Cincinnati, Ohio, which lies just north of what was known as the Mason-Dixon line, an imaginary line drawn in the 1760s that originally separated Maryland from Delaware. It was later extended past Ohio, Indiana, Illinois, and Missouri. The line was first created to settle a dispute between William Penn and Charles Calver over a strip of land between the two states. It also served to distinguish southern slaveholding states from northern "free" states before the Civil War. Cincinnati was also one of the stops along the Underground Railroad, the route that slaves used to move from southern states to escape the constant threat of lynching and other terrible things. Now it's the home of the National Underground Railroad Freedom Center.

Cincinnati was also the destination of poor southern Whites moving north to work in the Cincinnati factories. They brought with them their hatred of Black folks, instilled in them by the southern aristocracy. This hate kept them from mixing with southern

Blacks. Combined, the two groups would have been a threat, but as long as the oligarchs could keep the former slaves and poor whites separated and feeling the other was a threat, both groups could be controlled.

The result was a tumultuous and often violent mix of poor Whites and descendants of southern slaves. Between the two groups, there was an ongoing undeclared war, reminiscent of the Civil War era, that refused to die even with the passing of generations. Both groups carried with them all the hatred, resentment, and prejudices they had held against each other in their former locations.

This was a no-win situation for either of these two groups, for although many of these White folks thought they were better than us, they weren't going to get invited to the party either. They were, and still are, pawns, being used by the ruling class to do their bidding. As long as the aristocracy is successful in convincing low-income Whites that Blacks and other minorities are the source of their troubles, neither group will make significant progress.

Chapter 2

MY DAD

M Y FATHER CAME NORTH from Lapine, a small town in southern Alabama. About five foot eight inches in height, good looking and a sharp dresser. Always sporting sharp creased pants, sometimes with suspenders— sometimes not, long-sleeved tucked in shirts with a pipe hanging from the side of his mouth which was sometimes lit but mostly not, he carried himself with a confidence that was contagious to everyone around him. My dad was a self-described "skinflint" and could squeeze three nickels from a dime. Nothing went to waste in our house and he would even suck the marrow out of a chicken bone to make sure nothing was wasted. He was part of the Great Migration of Blacks from 1916 to 1970, following the promise of freedom and equality in the northern cities. He was a smart man but was relegated to a janitorial position at one of the local manufacturing plants.

Sometimes we'd ask him about the town he came from, his mom, his dad, and his childhood. He never gave us direct answers, only saying things like, "You don't want to know about where I came from" or "The past needs to be left in the past." Then he'd change the subject. It wasn't until many years later, while reading Isabel Wilkerson's *The Warmth of Other Suns*, that I learned about the conditions small-town southern Blacks suffered during those times, and I came to understand why he wanted the past to be left alone. His experience in the South was obviously much too painful for him to want to recall. Despite the racial climate of the times and economic barriers, he managed to support a wife and five kids and at the same time buy our family house in Evanston, Cincinnati and two rental houses.

One of my earliest memories is of walking with my dad through downtown Cincinnati near Fountain Square in the heart of the city. It was a drab southern Ohio day, and the sidewalks were filled with people. We had been walking for a while when I spotted a water fountain and headed over for a drink. My dad quickly pulled me away, saying, "You can't drink from that one."

Looking up at him, I asked, "Why?"

He looked down at me and said, "That's for White people."

I couldn't understand what he meant—there was a water fountain that worked, and I saw other people drinking from it, so why couldn't I?

That incident impacted me so much that I still remember it vividly. I remember the sharply creased pants, gray wool coat, and Stetson hat my dad was wearing and the corduroy parka and little Oxford shoes I was wearing.

I remember the water fountain with the "Whites Only" sign.

I remember the embarrassment of my father trying to explain the difference in class, privilege, and status between us and White people, and why this meant they had certain privileges and we didn't. What I remember most, though, was the difficulty my dad had in trying to explain this to me and at the same time hold his head high and serve as a role model for his son.

This memory is a part of me and always will be. It is burned into my consciousness and has helped shape who I am and how I feel about this country and my place in it. I was too young to understand the significance of it at the time, though obviously it must have affected me greatly, as I keep revisiting it again and again throughout my life. Like peeling back layers of an onion, every time I revisit it, I find new meanings, new feelings. It is a constant reminder of inequality stamped in my psyche.

That one little incident serves as a reminder of the overall attitude of Whites toward Blacks at the time. It was not questioned or challenged, but just accepted as the way of things. By law, we have moved beyond that, but we all know there are still many out there who would accept and even promote going back to those times if given the chance. It's a reminder that the fight for equality is constant and must go on. We cannot rest and assume things are okay, as we did for a short time from 2008 to 2016. The election of 2016 and the resurrection of the white supremacy movement since then is the result of that idleness, and our democracy has suffered greatly for it.

Chapter 3

FORBIDDEN LOVE 1905

M Y GRANDPARENTS, WILLIAM SMITH and Martha Ann Walton, moved to Cincinnati from Louisa, Virginia, a small town in northeastern Virginia that had grown up around the cultivation of tobacco. It was a tidy little town with a main street lined with well-kept shops, and the sweet aroma of tobacco was always thick in the air. There was of course the church where residents could go every Sunday to celebrate the goodness of the Lord and give thanks for all they had. If you asked any of the White residents of Louisa county, they would say, "All is well," and it was—for them. The town folk exuded the sweet, genteel mannerisms endemic to southern hospitality; a thick façade that masked the horrific deeds that had enabled them to enjoy the privileged lifestyle they enjoyed. Just as thick was the institutional racism: inescapable and ever-present, like an old, ugly suit that should have been discarded long ago.

If you asked the Black folks, they'd tell you about the weight of the souls of generations of slaves who had toiled and died under the unrelenting sun with no reward. They would tell you of the blood and tears that fertilized the profitable tobacco harvests, with no benefit to themselves—the sole beneficiary being the plantation owners. They would tell you about the daughters who were forcibly taken from their parents in the dark of night and raped by plantation owners, their sons, or whatever White man wanted to, while the girls' mothers, fathers, sisters, and brothers listened to their screams with no recourse. They would tell you about the young boys sold off to other plantations with their mothers helplessly crying long into the night.

The juxtaposition of these two worlds occupying the same space with such different histories exists even into the 21st century. The southern hospitality rings false when seen in this context. The rationalizations and lies were a narrative repeated constantly to justify the unspeakable things the Whites had done to generations of Black families. The collective, selective memory of the White residents of Louisa does not include the reality so fresh in the minds of the Black residents.

I understand that not all White people participated in these horrors, and descendants of these slave owners should not have to suffer for the sins of their fathers and grandfathers, unless they continue with those sins. But the horrible history is there, and we don't know what to do with it.

Following the end of the Civil War and the Emancipation Proclamation, many of the former slaves became sharecroppers, renting small plots of land and growing crops to be sold to the plantation owners. For most there was no alternative. They had nothing else to fall back on, having worked on plantations their entire lives. They had been forbidden to learn to read or write. They had no money and no concept of finance or of how to survive in this White man's world. What little they knew about this foreign land was learned while in the fields, which wasn't going to help. It was the equivalent of throwing someone who couldn't swim overboard without a life jacket.

Sharecropping amounted to little more than slavery; the small plots of land did not produce enough income to provide food and clothing, so they had to borrow from the landowner and were therefore constantly in debt to them therefore trapping them in debt and poverty for their remaining life, sometimes having to pass the debt on to future generations. Challenging the system could lead to violence, imprisonment, or even death.

There was a glimmer of hope when William Tecumseh Sherman and President Lincoln promised forty acres and a mule to emancipated Blacks, but this promise was quickly rescinded by the next administration, and the parcels that had been doled out were forcefully taken back by Whites. Plantations were returned to their former owners by law and by force. To this day, thirty-five to forty-five percent of the wealth in this country is inherited, and real estate remains the largest segment of household wealth. The foundations so many White families would base their wealth on for generations was denied these former slaves and their descendants, forcing them to operate at a deficit that to this day we have never recovered from.

***

"Punishment for marriage.—If any white person intermarry with a colored person, or any colored person intermarry with a white person, he shall be guilty of a felony and shall be punished by confinement in the penitentiary for not less than one nor more than five years."

—Excerpt from Virginia Miscegenation Laws, Section 20-59 of the Virginia Code (1950)

To say that nineteenth and twentieth century Virginia was a hostile environment for interracial relationships could be considered the understatement of the century. The laws of Virginia at the time inferred that the African American race was so inferior that it was a felony to allow White blood to be polluted by Black blood.

The anti-miscegenation laws were one thing, and bad enough, but outside of the law was where the punishment was most severe. Black men or even Black boys were hanged or beaten for small infractions, such as looking in the direction of a White woman too long or talking back to a White man. The hanging of Black males was cause for celebration among Whites of the time and was advertised much as one would advertise a musical concert or circus: families would bring picnic baskets and settle in for the show. They'd bring their children to watch the spectacle and to begin their indoctrination so that they too would know how to treat niggers who were "out of line." They would take pictures of themselves next to the dead Black boy hanging from a tree and make postcards to send to friends and relatives. They even sold pieces of the lynched boy's clothing as souvenirs.

And they called themselves "civilized."

This is the environment William and Martha Ann found themselves in. William, a tall, lanky, athletic-looking young man with skin as black as coal, lived in the house of the Walton family. He had no memory of his mother or father. The owners of the house, Joseph and Eliza Walton, were the closest he had ever come to having parents, as he had lived and worked there for as long as he could remember.

Martha, a pretty, young southern belle with strawberry blond hair, pale white skin, and bright blue eyes, was the daughter of Joseph and Eliza Walton. Martha Ann could trace her family tree back to England, from where her ancestors migrated to the Americas in the seventeenth century. William's search would stop at him.

Somehow, whether it was natural attraction, proximity, or just plain love, they found themselves in the extremely dangerous position of being a Black man and White woman in love—in the deep South, in Louisa County, Virginia.

Of course, showing their affection was out of the question. Louisa was a town of around 350 at the time, and, as in any small town, everyone knew everyone else's business. Everything they did had to be secretive: no dates, no walks in the park, no visible displays of affection, no love notes for fear of being caught—the consequences would have been severe. Covert kisses, adoring glances in passing, and secretive embraces had to suffice. Over time, their love swelled like a dammed river threatening to burst its banks. Theirs was a love that transcended all physical and institutional bounds.

Faced with the possibility of imprisonment or even death, they had no other alternative but to flee north, where there was at least the possibility of being able to marry. So, one balmy June night in 1905, they set a course north toward the alluring prospect of finding a place where they could freely express their love for each other without recrimination. Martha Ann took more traditional modes of transportation, and William followed the remnants of the Underground Railroad and the Green Book, as so many former slaves and disenfranchised Black folks were doing and had done before him.

The journey for William was fraught with danger; there were few, if any, opportunities for lodging and food along the way. He had to rely on word of mouth from Black folks who had made the journey before him. Some of the information was accurate, but some was not. This was the era of Jim Crow laws, enacted to prevent African Americans from mixing with members of the White race. These laws included such things as:

"It shall be unlawful for a negro and white person to play together or in company with each other in any game of cards or dice, dominoes or checkers."—**Birmingham, Alabama, 1930**

"Any person...presenting for public acceptance or general information, arguments or suggestions in favor of social equality or of intermarriage between whites and negroes, shall be guilty of a misdemeanor and subject to a fine not exceeding five hundred dollars or imprisonment not exceeding six months or both fine and imprisonment in the discretion of the court."—**Mississippi, 1920**

"Any white woman who shall suffer or permit herself to be got with child by a negro or mulatto...shall be sentenced to the penitentiary for not less than eighteen months." —**Maryland, 1924**

Clearly there was fear among Whites of being touched or even being in the vicinity of Blacks, much less allowing a Black man to have intimate relations with a White woman. They even had penalties for anyone who was presumptuous enough to suggest a Black person should be socially equal to a White person.

They met up again in Rossmoyne, Ohio, a suburb of Cincinnati. Although they were across the Mason-Dixon line, this is not to say they were free from discrimination. Ohio had repealed its anti-miscegenation laws, but the Klan was active in the area, and mixing of the races was as unacceptable to them as it was to many Whites of that time.

Against all odds they were married in or around 1908, bought a farm, and raised three daughters and a son. He, being the consummate entrepreneur, started the bus line for the area and operated it successfully for many years. Legend says the Ku Klux Klan called him one day, asking if they could use his buses to transport members to one of their meetings. His reply was, "Sure, I don't have a problem with that, but I'm gonna drive to make sure ya'll don't mess up my buses."

I don't know if this is legend or truth, but I do know he was so big that the house shook when he walked up the stairs, and he was not someone you would want to be on the wrong side of.

Their story closely mirrors what the Lovings went through in 1967 in Virginia, which led to the Supreme Court decision that struck down all state laws banning interracial marriage as violations of the equal protection and due process clauses of the Fourteenth Amendment to the U.S. Constitution—only this was more than fifty years before the Loving case, and no Supreme Court was going to stand up for them.

William and Martha must have had incredible strength to be able to withstand the pressures of being an interracial couple in a nation that so strongly discouraged the intermingling of races. Their situation is a testament to the fact that true love crosses all barriers.

My mother never talked about being raised in a multiracial family, but it surely must have raised eyebrows. My family just didn't talk much about things like that. We weren't raised to consciously see race as a factor in a person's worth, even though when we stepped outside the door, it was a factor to others. I don't know, maybe it was an embarrassment, but not to us. I think we were embarrassed for people who believed the fallacy that they were better than us because of the color of their skin.

In my parents' view, White people should have evolved enough to feel confident within themselves without the crutch of having to look down on someone else in order to feel good about themselves. I'm sure some of them even believed the myth of White superiority that had been perpetuated, just as some people do to this day, but intelligent people should know better.

It wasn't until much later in my life that what my parents instilled in me began to take effect, but they had planted the seeds. When the time was right for the seeds to sprout, I had the foundation they had built for me: I could be whatever I chose to be if I made the commitment and put in the work to achieve my goals and dreams.

My parents taught me —and I still believe— that racial stereotypes are in other people's minds and are myths created by those in power to maintain the advantages they've enjoyed over the centuries here in the United States. Advantages that have put Black people at a distinct disadvantage that we are still trying to overcome.

Times are changing. I'm glad they are. More and more people are beginning to question and challenge stereotypes, and one by one, they are being swept away as they should be. We've come a long way since Whites-only water fountains, but we still have so far to go.

Chapter 4

THE HOOD

We lived in a two-bedroom house into which we managed to cram seven people. My four sisters shared the two actual bedrooms, my mom and dad slept in what was designed to be the dining room, and I slept in what must have been a leftover space under the eaves that the builder couldn't figure out what to do with. It was at the top of the stairs, with no door and a slanted ceiling that allowed for around four feet of standing room. My bedroom was also right next to the one and only bathroom in the house. Anyone going to the bathroom had to go through my room. My bed was four feet away from the bathroom door, so I knew everyone's business. It was a cozy house to say the least, but it was our home, and we appreciated having it.

Our snug little house sat on the corner of Potter Place and Woodburn Avenue, and it was bordered by the railroad tracks in back and G.A. Gray Manufacturing Company on one side. I never knew what they did at that factory; I just remember that a bunch of White men would arrive in the morning with determined looks on their faces and lunchboxes in hand. They'd make a lot of noise all day and then leave at night with empty lunchboxes and the same determined look on their faces. They never acknowledged our existence, walking past us as if we were invisible, phantoms in our own neighborhood. It was as if they resented the fact that we were there.

My friends and I staged boxing matches, which sometimes turned into fights, and when we got tired of beating on each other, we made the younger kids fight each other. Some of them grew up to be neighborhood terrors because they grew up fighting and got good at it.

Sometimes our summer days started like this: We'd all get up in the morning, meet at one of our houses, and decide what we were going to do that day: explore the neighborhood or another neighborhood, ride bikes, walk the storm sewers or railroad tracks—whatever. But our favorite way to start summer days was watching "THE IMMACULATE BOOTY." It belonged to the lady who lived across the street from my friend Ernest's house. We'd gather on Ernest's front porch steps, waiting for her to appear. Beetle, Ernest, Spunky, and I, four thirteen-year-olds, anxiously waited for "the event."

The doorknob turned, the door opened, and she would appear at the entrance, pause for a minute, and begin the walk to her car. Up until that time, we'd been joking and jostling each other, but when she began the walk, all talking ceased, time stood still, and all our focus was solely on The Immaculate Booty—taking in every bounce, every jiggle, every nuance it produced as she made the short walk to her car. It was only twenty-five or so feet from the front door to her car, but it seemed like a mile and an eternity to us.

The movement wasn't side to side; it wasn't up and down; it was a kind of circular movement with a little jiggle at the end of each step that made the Booty seem as if it had a life of its own. It wasn't overly large but by no means small; it looked firm but had a sufficient amount of bounce. It was as if it was disconnected from everything else and dropped here on earth just for our enjoyment.

It didn't matter what else was happening in the world: the stock market could crash, aliens could invade Earth, and the rest of the world could implode and fall to pieces around us, but for those thirty seconds, our world was perfect.

When she got to her car, she'd slide in gracefully, close the door, and give us a little sideways smile as she drove away. I'm sure she knew it was no coincidence that we happened to be on the front steps every morning when she made the walk to her car. In our minds, she added a little extra jiggle just for our benefit—or maybe she didn't even notice us. I don't know, but she was the highlight of our day and a great way to begin our summer days.

***

"To his dog, every man is Napolean; hence the constant popularity of dogs."
—Aldous Huxley

HOUND DOG

An integral part of our neighborhood was Hound Dog. My best friend, confidant, constant companion, and protector; all these things described Hound Dog. Part boxer and part pit bull and all badass. He had long, tattered ears and a short tail. He was built like a tank, with a broad, muscular chest, a wide face, and powerful jaws. All muscle and not an ounce of fat, he was the canine combo of Arnold Schwarzenegger and Claude Van Damme. He was slightly bowlegged and walked with a swagger that said, "I'm the baddest creature on four legs." Although he was my best friend, he was not to be confined by a leash. The one time I tried putting him on a leash, I found myself being dragged face-first down the sidewalk until I finally let go.

Wherever I went, he went. I spent more time talking to him than to anyone else—and I swear he understood. If I was in trouble, he was the one who would come and sit by my side to comfort me. Sometimes after everyone was in bed, he'd jump up on my bed, but he knew enough to jump down before anyone came up the stairs and caught him. I usually woke up in the morning to him licking my face, telling me it was time to start the day.

If I was out of town, he'd hang with the gang, which meant that if something went down around the neighborhood, and Hound Dog was spotted in the area, the cops assumed I was involved. They would show up at the house asking for me and I'd have some explaining to do. Yes, they knew Hound Dog, too.

He was the most lovable dog you'd ever want to know, but if there was a threat to me or anyone on our block, he would be right there as our greatest defender. His deep growl was enough to scare off any would-be burglar, and if he didn't like you or sensed bad intentions, he'd let you know in no uncertain terms.

In my early teens, I spent more time with Hound Dog than anyone else. We'd hit the little patch of woods by the railroad tracks where he'd scare up a rabbit, and the chase would be on. Sometimes, if we were lucky, Hound Dog would get close enough to grab it, or maybe I'd bean the rabbit with a good-sized rock.

I'd pack a lunch for both of us in the morning and hit the streets with no destination in mind. Sometimes we'd end up on the other side of town, then find our way back in time for supper. Our adventures were between the two of us, with no need to share them with anyone else.

Tadpole Pond was one of our waypoints. It was a shallow pond created by a break in the storm sewer pipes and surrounded by maples and oaks. In the summer, we caught tadpoles and bluegill. In the winter, when it froze over enough for us to walk on, us neighborhood kids would gather for a spirited game of ice hockey, using broken branches for hockey sticks and a round rock for the puck. We didn't have skates; we just slid around in our boots, pretending they were skates. Our games would sometimes get pretty wild with no referee around to call fouls, so we had fouls aplenty.

During one of our more lively games, sticks were flying—not necessarily always aimed at the puck—when suddenly one of the members of the opposing team went down. It took a second to register what had happened, but then I realized Hound Dog had taken him down. He thought the guy was attacking me with the stick, and the only thing that saved him was that he had three layers of clothing on, and Hound Dog couldn't quite get his teeth through all the layers. We had to take a time-out while I assured Hound Dog the guy meant no harm to me.

Since there were no leash laws back in those days, dogs ran free, and riding bikes through other neighborhoods was an adventure. Some dogs were attracted by bikes and their riders and would take up the chase when we rode by. We'd pedal hard to build up speed and hold our feet up out of range when they charged. Hound Dog kept pace with us and ran interference. If a dog took up the chase, Hound Dog would come up from behind, take down the offending canine, give him a proper ass-kicking, and catch up with us later.

One afternoon, we were sitting on our porch when a neighborhood tough guy, Larry Rowland, decided to bring his huge German shepherd mix, Chico, over. Larry was older than us, big for his age and a nice guy, until you crossed him—then he became your worst nightmare. He had oversized biceps and would let us hang on them, one from each arm, without any sign of strain.

It was important to Larry that he had the baddest dog to match his badass reputation. His Chico also ruled the roost most times, but this day proved to be Chico's undoing. Larry was walking by the house when Chico spotted Hound Dog. With some encouragement from Larry, Chico decided to take him on. Chico charged with a roar, hackles raised and teeth bared. We all scrambled out of the way, except for Hound Dog, who rose from the porch, grabbed Chico by the neck, and threw him through our glass storm door. Crash! Glass and aluminum parts scattered everywhere. That's all it took.

Chico scrambled to get as far away from Hound Dog as his paws could carry him—and that was the end of it!

Many years later I learned Larry met his demise when he decided to take on three young gangbangers, and they beat him to death. Everyone said Larry held his own and left his mark on the gangbangers, but nevertheless, Larry was dead—he crawled into an abandoned building and died alone. He was sixty-five years old and had no business still trying to prove himself, but old habits die hard.

Hound Dog was somewhat of a free spirit and would sometimes disappear for days at a time, probably chasing some girl dog or something. He'd often come back bleeding from multiple wounds. They were battle scars; it was just his way. Then one day he left on one of his excursions and never returned.

For months I searched the woods, the streets, and everywhere I thought he might be, but I never found him. The neighborhood mourned him, our protector and my best friend. For me, there will never be another dog like him, and he just gets bigger and badder in his reputation as time goes by.

On a recent trip to Cincinnati, more than fifty years later, some of the guys from the old neighborhood were sitting around drinking whiskey and talking about the good old days, when there was a pause, and someone said, "Hound Dog, man, what a dog—there will never be another one like him."

***

My uncle Joe lived around the corner from us at the end of Brewster Avenue, a dead-end street terminating in a patch of woods. Uncle Joe was a giant of a man who loved to hunt and fish. He was always dressed in old farmer-johns, frayed around the edges, and high-top hunting boots. He'd sometimes stand outside my window and throw rocks to wake me to go hunting with him.

One day, I was on my way to his house to help him feed his hound dogs. But when I rounded the corner and saw a fancy tour bus parked there, I forgot all about Uncle Joe and his dogs. It was a huge bus, the kind you saw on the highway carrying rich folks or famous musicians to their destinations, only there were no seats in this bus save for the driver's seat. Instead, it was packed with flashy costumes and clothing of all types, including a whole rack of fancy black satin capes. This could only mean one thing: James Brown and the Famous Flames were in town!

King Record Company was directly across the street from Uncle Joe's house. It was an old brick building with a chain link fence on one side. The place was plain and innocuous: no sign, no windows, just a plain building stuck in between a residential and an industrial area with no attempt at glitter. It was dedicated to the recording and production of the music of the times. This is where famous recording artists like Otis Redding, Hank Ballard, Ike Turner, and John Lee Hooker came to commit their music to vinyl for the world to hear.

At King Records, artists could record one day, press vinyl the next, and have a recording released to the public within a week, sometimes faster. There were fifty-five-gallon drums behind the studio into which they threw slightly warped records that weren't quality enough for stores. We would dig through the barrels until we found records good enough to play, and consequently we always got recordings from many of these artists before they hit the radio.

It wasn't like it is today. When these bands came to record it was totally low-key: no press and no groupies hanging at the door. In fact, most times no one even knew when they were in town—but when the tour bus was there, we knew.

My favorite was when James Brown and the Famous Flames came to town. I looked forward to the Flames as much as James Brown. They were three smooth-talking, immaculately dressed men. Everything about them reeked of style. They danced as if they were melded together, with synchronized moves and perfect harmonies, always on key. With spit-shined black Florsheim shoes, color coordination down to their cufflinks, and slicked-back hair always perfectly styled, they were as cool as anyone I'd ever seen.

Sometimes on breaks, the Flames would come out and hang out with us kids.

"Hey, kids, you wanna learn some moves?"

They'd practice their moves in the middle of the street and allow us kids to join them. These guys were consummate entertainers. We appreciated the attention they gave us, but we never asked for autographs or anything. I think we were so used to these artists being around that we took it for granted; we didn't know we were in the presence of greatness until much later in life. It wasn't unusual for them to come out of the studio on break and sit around with us, telling stories about their times on the road. This was probably one of the things that compelled me to pursue a life as a jazz and R&B singer later in life.

One afternoon we were hanging with Hank Ballard while he was sitting outside waiting for his taxi. He had just finished a recording session, and we could tell he was upset about something. We were peppering him with questions, and he finally confided in us that he was upset that Chubby Checker had recorded his own version of "The Twist" and had somehow taken most of the credit for creating the Twist craze.

"That was my song, my dance, man. Now everybody thinks Chubby Boy started it. But that's all right, you know, 'cause I've got some more good shit coming out—just watch me work."

Once in a while, if no one was watching, we were able to sneak inside the entrance of the studio; if we were real quiet and didn't get caught, we could witness the making of some of the most iconic R&B music of the times.

James Brown was such a perfectionist; he'd make the band play a lick over and over until it was perfect, so much so that we would eventually become bored with it and sneak back out. I was too young then to attend any of his concerts, but later in life I was able to see the results of his perfectionism. His concerts were a marvel in precision and timing. Everything from dance steps, to a toss of his head, to a cymbal crash, was precisely on time, and there was hell to pay if it wasn't.

This was just one of the many things I loved about growing up in Cincinnati and my neighborhood. Looking back, I realize that we didn't have much but there was never a dull moment, always something to do and I wouldn't change it for anything.

Chapter 5

RIDERS OF THE RAILS

W HERE MY BACKYARD ENDED, the railroad tracks began; I went to sleep to the sound of the train and awoke to the sound of the train. The train tracks were inviting, and even to this day I love trains and train tracks—the gleaming twin rails, the path to adventure.

This was the time of the old coal-burning steam engines. They were big black behemoths, loud and messy. The ground shook, and black ash spewed from their smokestacks as they passed. Everything in the neighborhood, from cars to my mother's laundry, always had a light coating of ash.

The huge locomotives were a thing of beauty. Their power was evident in the number of fully loaded boxcars and tankers they could pull. They would hook up to a full line of cars with a loud metallic thud, sending echoes down the line, and then they would start out with a mighty *chug, chug, chug-chug-chug* as the wheels slipped on the rails. Little by little the engine would gain traction and speed until we could hear the *clack, clack-clickety-clack* of the wheels passing over the gaps in the rails. Then came the little red caboose with the smokestack and woodstove to keep the crew warm. We'd always wave. Sometimes they'd wave back, sometimes not.

We spent many days walking the railroad tracks, balancing on the narrow rails, occasionally having to race across trestles to outrun oncoming trains, or we'd jump on a slow-moving train to ride to other parts of town, running alongside, grabbing a handrail, and swinging ourselves up on the train, being careful not to miss and end up under the wheels. If you started enjoying the ride too much and waited until the train had picked up too much speed, you had to make the decision to jump from the fast-moving train—or end up in parts unknown. The trick to getting off was to start running as fast as you could as soon as your feet hit the ground, trying to match your running speed to the speed of the train. If you didn't, momentum would take over, and you'd find yourself planted face-first on the roadbed of sharp rocks.

One day Ernest, for some strange reason, decided to just jump off a fast-moving train without running—a bad move. His feet hit the ground, and instantaneously his face was planted in the gravel. We checked to see if he was all right, then started laughing. No ...actually, we started laughing first. He was pissed, partly out of embarrassment but mostly because we were laughing so hard while he was lying there bleeding.

***

This was the '50s, and there were lots of hobos on the road in those days. Some panhandled on the streets, but most rode the rails from town to town, always looking for opportunities whether honest or dishonest. They had a code of ethics many of them followed. They'd do an honest day's work when it was available, but if a purse or wallet was left unattended, they would conveniently forget that part of the code, and it would end up in their bag. That was the hobo way of life.

There were hobo camps here and there along the railroad. This was their highway. Most of the camps were just lean-tos covered with canvas tarps and blankets. Some were more elaborate and permanent, with actual structures with tin roofs pilfered from construction sites, barbeque pits, clotheslines—the works. They functioned like little towns; that is, until the Pinkerton Railroad Detectives (the Bulls) discovered them and tore them down. Most times they timed their raids for early in the morning before the hobos woke up or late at night when they were asleep, then they'd wade in with their clubs swinging. It was pandemonium as the hobos scrambled, trying to grab what they could and get out before they got knocked upside the head. Then the Bulls would level the camp and everything in it.

We had mixed feelings about the destruction of these camps. On one hand, the hobos were fellow inhabitants of the twin rails and the culture that came along with it; on the other hand, they sometimes felt like we were competition and would chase us when they caught sight of us. A lot of the sense of adventure and alternative lifestyle I lived later in life is no doubt a result of watching these guys play out their roles in life.

I thought of them as not-so-noble outlaws, sorta like Robin Hood, but stealing from the rich and keeping it for themselves. At the same time, they were people to be feared because we were sometimes after the same spoils they were, and if they caught us, they would probably have given us a good ass-kicking...but avoiding them was part of the fun of it!

To this day, when I hear the 12:30 a.m. train whistle through my bedroom window, that lonely whistle takes me right back to my childhood by the railroad tracks; it envelopes me in all the sadness I've felt as well as the strength I have gained along the way. It reminds me of the good people I've known, and the bad, but more than anything else, it reminds me of "home."

The hobos always had a campfire going and would gather at sundown to share the wine they had begged, borrowed, and stolen during the day and to swap stories. Sometimes we'd hide on the perimeter of the camp and listen to them spin their tales. They were colorful characters with whopping tales of life on the road and the adventures and dangers that came with the lifestyle. Most of them were probably outright lies or at least extreme exaggerations, but nonetheless, they were good storytellers. I always marveled how they could cradle a gallon jug of Thunderbird wine in the crook of their elbow and take a swig without missing a line of their storytelling.

One hot August evening we were hiding in the brush outside of one of the hobo camps, listening to their yarns. It was almost sundown and the light was low enough that they couldn't see us. They had a good fire going and were sitting around telling hobo stories.

Typically, whoever had the stage also had possession of the jug. That night, the storyteller was a short, scruffy hobo with old high-top boots that looked to be a size too large, tattered wide-brim brown felt hat with a feather in the hatband, and weathered skin like an old leather boot. The light from the fire made the cracks and creases in his face stand out even more, making him look like a character from a Charles Dickens novel. He was animated in a drunken sort of way, waving his hands, dancing in a wine-induced swaying, weaving hobo ballet but always managing to keep on his feet. He was in the middle of his story, and it was a good one, so everyone was paying rapt attention.

He was lifting the jug to his lips, when Spunky, who had incredibly good aim, rose, flung a rock, and broke the jug. Kablam! Broken glass and cheap wine flew all over the camp. It took us by surprise because we hadn't known Spunky was going to do it, but the reaction from the camp brought us back to the moment.

There was a pause. Then one of them spotted us, and all hell broke loose as they gave chase.

Wine was a precious liquid to these guys, and messing with their wine was like talking bad about somebody's momma or touching a pimp's "'do." All we heard was "I'm gonna kill those damn kids!!"

We started running, tearing through the brush and tripping over each other trying to escape—we were laughing so hard we could barely run. We knew we had really pissed those guys off, and who knows what they would have done to us if they had caught us. It was touch-and-go for a minute. Ernest tripped, and we had to go back and help him. They were almost on us as we broke out of the woods and onto the railroad bed, but once we were on level ground, we were able to put some distance between them and us. Luckily, the hobos already had a good buzz going, so watching them stumble over each other was hilarious. They were already drunk, and that was probably the only thing that saved us.

I don't know why Spunky threw the rock, but it destroyed any relationship we had with the hobos. From then on, we had to watch our backs.

Spunky went on to be awarded the Medal of Honor while serving in Vietnam. I never found out what he did to earn it, but I assumed he must have thrown a hand grenade and saved a platoon or something.

***

Our neighborhood, Evanston, was integrated, with some Whites, some Blacks, and some Puerto Ricans, but we all hung out together. Pickup basketball games, cowboys and Indians, stoop ball—we played 'til the sun went down. When my mom cooked a peach cobbler, it didn't matter what color you were; you were going to end up sitting on my front porch, licking your fingers.

Little by little, though, it was changing. Most of the Whites were moving out of the neighborhood, and more Black folks were moving in. It happened over time, slow and subtle, and in our naïvete, we didn't take much notice of the changeover.

Ricky was just part of the gang. He ran with us and played sports with us, and we all walked to school together. In our minds, he was no different than us. He was White, but we never gave it a second thought.

Then one day we were sitting on my front porch and saw a moving van pull up to Ricky's house—and poof, Ricky was gone. No goodbyes, no, "This is our new address, drop in whenever you want," no nothing—just gone. We thought, surely, he would visit, come over for a game of ball, check in with us to see what was going on in the old neighborhood, but there was nothing.

A couple of years went by, and we had gotten over the sudden departure. Then, one hot summer day, we were in the street playing a rowdy game of football when out of the corner of my eye, I saw Ricky and his dad approaching. They were back for a visit of the old neighborhood. I could see his dad pointing out houses and commenting on how it used to be. We were excited to see our old friend Ricky. We called out, "Hey Ricky!" But to our amazement, Ricky and his dad just walked past us as if we were ghosts; they didn't even look in our direction!

We looked at each other as if to validate we had all experienced the same thing—yes, we had. We tried to get into the game again but ended up just milling around for a bit. None of us felt like playing anymore, and we all just drifted home.

I told my mother what had happened. She got that knowing look on her face, the look I had seen on the faces of so many old Black folks when they'd been dissed in some way or other. She said, "Ricky is with his own kind now. He doesn't have much use for us anymore."

It was a deep hurt that stuck with me for a long time. At first, I was sad that Ricky didn't acknowledge me as a friend anymore, but as I got older and understood what Ricky had done and why, I became angry with him for succumbing to this race thing. I thought our friendship was bigger than that; I felt a friendship should be able to overcome racial differences. His whiteness didn't mean anything to us when he lived in our neighborhood, and we had assumed he felt the same. What had changed? I wondered if his parents and new friends pressured him into changing his attitude toward us. I wondered if there was some little inkling of remorse somewhere in his soul, an unsettling feeling something was wrong about his new attitude. I'll never know. I never saw Ricky again.

My family was probably the least race-conscious family you would ever meet. I grew up accepting people for who they were, not judging by what race or religion they were or what country they were from. I didn't understand then, and I still have trouble grasping the concept of hating someone you've never met based on the color of their skin, who they worshiped or whatever. When I get the "look" from someone passing on the street or hear a racial epithet aimed in my direction, I'm still caught off guard and find myself wondering, "Do I know that person? Did I do something to offend them?"

One of my most perplexing moments was when I learned some White people hated Jewish people. To me, Jewish people were White people, too.

"You mean they hate each other, too? I thought they just hated us! What the hell is wrong with these people?"

I'm not totally naive; I know racial hatred exists—you can't help but acknowledge it. It's the logic behind it that still escapes me. After all, people of European descent brought Africans to this country against their will, held them as slaves, raped their women, beat them, killed them, and committed all kinds of atrocities against these Africans and their descendants. Logic says we should be the ones doing the hating, not the other way around, but I understand that the aristocracy in this nation would rather have Blacks and working-class Whites be against each other—it makes it easier for them to keep control. It's incongruous that Black folks and White folks have bought into it and allowed it to keep them separate with such hostility toward each another for so long.

***

"Pit race against race, religion against religion, prejudice against prejudice. Divide and conquer! We must not let that happen here."
——**Eleanor Roosevelt**

We had other White friends in the neighborhood: the Alfords. Our families always enjoyed each other's company and would regularly meet for dinner or to just to get together. As the neighborhood continued changing over, it wasn't long before the Alfords also moved across the tracks to Norwood. Norwood was all White, whereas Evanston, for all intents and purposes, had become all Black. If we went down to Norwood, we knew we were probably going to have to fight, and vice versa. Why? Because we were Black and they were White, and we were supposed to hate each other—sounds stupid when you say it, doesn't it?

We continued to be good friends with the Alfords and would sometimes go over to their house for dinner. The deal was, though, we had to go after nightfall, pull into their driveway all the way back to where the garage was, and enter through the back door, making sure none of their neighbors saw us. If we had been seen entering their house through the front door in broad daylight, and it came to light that the Alfords had Black friends, they would have been driven from the neighborhood. And when they came to visit us, they had to make sure none of their White friends or neighbors knew they were going to visit Black friends.

I think back on that now and realize just how absurd it was. What business is it of anyone else who we socialized with? It's frustrating when you think about how people acted back then, but even more exasperating when you realize that type of situation is still being played out in certain parts of the country.

Lots of folks made fun of Rodney King when he made the statement, "Can we all get along?" But as simple as it sounded, I guess I must ask the same question:

"Why can't we just get along?"

Chapter 6

CHURCH ON SUNDAY

My Failed Indoctrination into Christianity

"*A MAN'S ETHICAL BEHAVIOR should be based effectually on sympathy, education and social ties and needs; no religious basis is necessary. Man would indeed be in a poor way if he had to be restrained by fear of punishment and hope of reward after death.*"

—Albert Einstein

I was raised in the African Methodist Episcopal Church. Allen Temple A.M.E. was a warm, nurturing environment. The church was full of like-minded people who looked out for each other and helped others in need. I still love the feeling the church provided, and I smile when I think about the people of Allen Temple A.M.E Church.

Allen Temple occupied an elaborate stucco building with colorful stained-glass windows and soaring cathedral ceilings adorned with angels and other deities. We sat in well-worn black lacquered pews, all focused on the pulpit. At the front of the auditorium was a massive pipe organ that filled the auditorium with the wonderful melodic chords endemic of traditional Christian hymns.

Our Sundays started downstairs with Sunday School, where I learned the different books of the Bible. It was usually led by a young woman of the congregation who was an ardent student of the Bible. I could feel the devotion emanating from her as she read the Bible to us impressionable little ones. However, I never could relate to any of these Bible verses; it was like they were stuck in a different time and place and did not apply to anything I was experiencing in my life. To me the Bible was full of long-dead characters in lands far away, who did nonsensical things and spoke in weird dialects.

From there, we moved up into the main auditorium. Of course, all the women were dressed to the nines with their finest dresses and the most elaborate hats you'd ever laid eyes on. Us guys were decked out in freshly pressed suits, spit-shined shoes, and pants with creases so sharp you could cut yourself on them. No sport coats or casual sweaters in those days; it was all Sunday go-to-meeting clothes. People who worked in other people's homes or factories during the week were transformed into finely attired princes and princesses on Sundays.

Our preacher, Reverend Drummer, was a master of the sermon. He was a tall, good-looking man, always immaculately dressed, with a warm and friendly demeanor. He was a good man, and I always had and still have a warm place in my heart for him. Reverend Drummer had a deep, booming voice loud enough that he didn't really need a microphone. He would start his sermon in a conversational tone, talking about a book of the Bible and explaining its significance. Lots of times, he would be casually leaning against the pulpit as if he were standing on his porch talking to his next-door neighbor. Then the tension would start building. He'd begin pacing the floor, his eyes taking on a feverish intensity as if there was a fire burning within. His voice would get louder, more percussive, and people would begin to get edgy in their seats; murmurs of "Amen" interspersed with "Yes, Lord" would emanate from the flock. This would encourage him, and his voice would rise, sometimes ending a phrase with, "Let me hear you say Amen!" And a chorus of Amens would come back at him.

One of the highlights of the service was the fat lady who sat in the pew in front of us. It seemed like about every Sunday, midway through the sermon, she would fart. Not just any old squeaky fart, one of those deep, resounding ones that was amplified as it reverberated off of the smooth surface of the pew on which she sat. Most of the old folks pretended like they didn't hear it, but us kids would start laughing to the point where I would get the dagger eyes from my mom, which meant, "You are about to get a whoopin' if you keep it up!"

Allen Temple was across the street from White Castle Burgers, which I loved dearly for their occasional coupons. You could get twelve burgers for a dollar—and it was right around the corner from the soda bar. Miraculously, right about the time the church service got to be boring, most of the young folk would have feigned an urgent need to visit the bathroom, and one by one we would leave the service and meet outside. Once we had gathered, we'd head over to White Castle or the soda bar around the corner. That's when the fun began.

Sometimes, though, I would stay back and listen to the sermon if it seemed like it had some significance. I was especially interested in the Old Testament, as I still am. A lot of what I got out of the New Testament was that we're all sinners, but don't worry, 'cause if you accept Jesus into your life, everything is all right.

Occasionally, some of my friends and I would go to Little Abraham's Bible Way Church of God in Christ. It was in an old theater building up the street from my house. Little Abraham was a handsome, smooth-talking preacher with enough charisma to fill a football stadium. Little Abe was the consummate cool dude—like Super Fly with a Bible.

Little Abe's band was one of the hottest bands in town. There was a Hammond B3 organist playing full-fat gospel chords, a bass guitar player, and a drummer laying down some seriously syncopated backbeats. Once they started rocking with the beat, it was hard to keep your seat.

When Little Abe entered the auditorium, the band would start getting down with something that only could be described as a mix of funk and gospel. By this time, the choir would be rocking at the back of the church, and then on signal they would start half-stepping down the aisle to the beat of the band while at the same time belting out one of those percussive hard-hitting gospel tunes that made you want to stand up and shout. There was tension in the air; something was coming that was about to rock everyone's world.

Then Little Abe stepped on stage, wearing a perfectly tailored white suit—everything matched and reeked of style, fashion, and quality. When he started in on his sermon, his voice was perfectly cadenced to bring out the emotion in the room. He could bring tears to the most hardened hoodlum's eyes, and make you want to jump up, confess, and give him all your money. Little Abe was sweet!

We were a bunch of little hoodlums sitting in the back of the church. We would put money in a hat, saying whoever got happy first would get it all. We had a couple guys who hung with us who really needed the money.

"How much money is in there, man?" Mike asked.

"Two whole dollars and some change, man—you feelin' it?"

"Not yet. Lemme know when there's three dollars in there."

When there was enough money in the hat, Mike would spring from his pew, shouting, "Praise the Lord, praise Jesus!" and start going into convulsions, talking in tongues, and all of the actions that coincided with getting happy. The sisters would converge on Mike, stand him up, all the while fanning him, saying, "Praise the Lord, praise Jesus." When he was done, he'd sit back down and say, "Gimme my money man."

***

All along, I felt something was missing in my religious and spiritual education, and I was curious about other religions and how other people practiced theirs, so I started visiting other churches.

I went to a Jewish synagogue, where I listened to the rabbi talk about the Old Testament but also about real-life stuff. There were no guilt trips, no fire and brimstone; you weren't going to hell if you didn't accept Jesus. They talked about things like how to manage yourself in the present world and interact with the rest of the world, you know—things you could really use. Mainly what I got from visiting Jewish temples was there is one God who wants us to do what is just and compassionate and for us to be good to each other. I found myself becoming jealous of them because they were being told they were okay, while we were being guilt-tripped into thinking we were all sinners.

I visited a "holy roller" church with my girlfriend, and man, they scared the shit out of me! People were flopping around on the floor, talking in tongues, and flailing around in the aisle. I was sitting in the congregation while she sang in the choir, when the man next to me suddenly flung out his arms and started yelling some crazy shit. He took me by surprise, and my natural reaction was to take him down before he got to me. I knocked his arm away and drew my fist back, but then I realized what was happening and settled back down in my seat. Nobody had really noticed what had almost gone down except my girlfriend. When I looked up at her, her eyes were as big as saucers. She gave me an earful about it later. She never invited me back, and I never went again.

I found a Buddhist temple and meditated with them to see if there was something I might be missing. I learned about Siddhartha, the Buddha, and the concepts of Karma, samsara, and enlightenment. It seemed more like a philosophy than a religion. I tried to decipher it and came back with a simple message: "Be good to everyone and everything." Sounds simple, doesn't it? I didn't stay with it long enough to understand it, but I learned enough to be intrigued and found myself returning to Buddhism later in life.

I visited St. Mark's Catholic Church, but everything was in Latin, and I didn't understand Latin—that didn't last long.

As a child and even as a teenager, going to church was not on top of my list of favorite things to do; in fact, it didn't even make the list. With the youth Bible studies, the weeklong church conferences, and all the things a life in the church demanded of you, I didn't see the sense in it. As nurturing as the church was, there were too many unanswered questions, and I couldn't just go on blind faith or someone else's concept of God.

I had voiced my aversion to going to church more than once, but it always fell on deaf ears. I think my parents must have thought that if I kept going to church and heard the same things over and over, it would finally stick. I asked questions about things the preacher said in his sermons. I read the Bible, compiled a list of questions, and received answers that were direct quotes from the same book I had questioned—none of which really answered my questions. I guess I was a lost cause, a preacher's nightmare.

Although Reverend Drummer didn't, some preachers have a way of making you feel guilty regardless of what you've done, sort of like the kid next door whose grandma gave him a whooping occasionally because "I know you did something wrong." I felt that the basis of Christianity was that we were guilty until proven innocent, starting with the premise that we are all sinners in some way or other, with only one way to resolve the issue of those sins: to accept Jesus into your life as the only salvation.

Just to clarify, I think Jesus was probably a very enlightened being who was here on earth to try and get us moving in the right direction. I'm sure he had good intentions, but I don't know what he really said, or what he would say if he were here today. I think he'd probably be embarrassed about things done in his name and say something like, "Can't we just get along?"

The Bible didn't quite answer my questions. They were words coming from people who had long since been dead. I wasn't even sure whose words they were, since the Bible had been rewritten, translated, and revised to suit King James and a host of others.

On one of my forays to the public library, I found a book about some of the major African cultures before European incursions. I learned of the many proud, rich cultures in Africa, including kingdoms like the ancient empire of Kush that stood as a regional power in Africa for over a thousand years and was an economic center with markets for ivory, incense, iron, and gold, and the Axum empire whose king commanded an army of over 200,000 warriors and that was a major player on the commercial route between the Roman Empire and India, and the kingdom of Mali whose king, Mansa Sundiata Keita, the Disney movie *The Lion King* was based on—and many other rich African cultures, deep cultures with their own religions and spiritualism.

I also read about how Europeans used religion to lull the Africans into passivity—and then one morning they woke up in chains. I learned how this systematic invasion was repeated in the Polynesian Islands, Australia, Fiji, Samoa, the Americas, and basically everywhere White Europeans landed.

How can I accept this religion? How can a race of people who were enslaved, tortured, raped, and killed adopt the very religion that led to their enslavement?

I came back with lots of questions, and I returned to my father, eager to discuss these ideas, which were new to me but old to the world. His every reply was a Bible verse, a proverb, or some other quote from the Bible, as if it were infallibly true, as if it explained everything, as if it was all I needed to know.

I was angry with him for not being able to go any deeper within himself and extract an answer from his heart.

I was angry with him because his heart had been taken over by this book, this religion that had been forced on our people to the point where they believed it was theirs.

And I was envious of him because that was all he needed.

He didn't need to go deep within himself for answers or contemplate the meaning of life, why we are here, or any of the existential concepts many of us deal with. It was all laid out for him and for all who chose to believe. The simplicity of this was profound. No matter what the question, the answer was in the book. No matter what the problem, the solution was in the book, and if you didn't believe him...READ THE DAMN BOOK!!!

Sometimes I wish it were that simple for me, to be able to accept this religion with all its teachings at face value. Ask for forgiveness and your sins are washed away; take it to the Lord in prayer and let him deal with it. But I can't. I'm just not built that way.

I tried probing my dad to see what else there was but to no avail. It was always a proverb or a Bible verse. My dad knew the Bible from front to back and back to front and could wield it like a sword.

He went to his grave believing these things, and I hope it was true for him.

When my mother was dying—and it wasn't an easy death for her—she called me one day and asked, "Why is God making me suffer like this? I've been a good Christian."

I had no answer for her. I wish I did. I wish I could have quoted a Bible verse that would have put her mind at ease. I wish I could have reminded her of a proverb that would explain her suffering and let her know there was some good in it. I wish I could have done something to help her maintain the strength and belief in God that had kept her strong her entire life, until now, during this last stage, as she began to question. I wanted her to go out believing, even though I didn't. Otherwise, all those years of faith, belief, and worship would have been for naught; but all I could say was, "I don't know."

History is full of people who have doubted their faith:

At the ninth hour, Jesus said, "Father, why hast thou forsaken me?" (Translation: *Dad, I did everything you said—what's with the cross, man?*)

Muhammad at first questioned the Revelation and was poised to leap from a cliff. (Translation: *This revelation stuff, it's just too much, man, so I'm just going to jump off this cliff.*)

Lao Tzu, fed up with God, humanity, and everything else, was on his way out when someone stopped him and said, "Hey, man, since you spent all of your life accumulating all this Godly wisdom, why don't you go on and write it down for us before you leave?" And so he wrote the Tao Te Ching.

Without bad we wouldn't know good; without darkness we wouldn't appreciate light; and without doubt we can't know faith. If you really want to know if you have faith, have it tested, and if you come out with your faith intact—that's when you know you have it.

In the end, my mom's faith was strong enough that she overcame her momentary doubt, and that is what matters. She died with her faith intact.

***

My dad and I were never able to see eye to eye on Christianity and the Bible and over time it became an insurmountable wedge between the two of us, leaving us unable to communicate without "going there." He accepted the teachings at face value and lived his life by them, while I questioned everything about Christianity. Actually—I think I questioned everything about everything.

It came to a head one day when I asked him for advice on some trivial thing, and he came back with a Bible verse. I exploded and said, "I don't want to hear some goddamn Bible proverb; I want to know what YOU think!"

Needless to say, this didn't go over well. It was pretty much the beginning of the end of our relationship. Our communication disintegrated from that point, and I left home thinking he didn't approve of me. So, being the stubborn, hardheaded young man I was, I lived up to my childhood nickname "Rockhead" and decided I didn't need his approval. I cut him off and moved on with my life with limited communication with him. We would exchange pleasantries but nothing deep. When I called home, if he answered the phone he'd invariably ask, "You goin' to church, boy?"

The answer was always "No."

And he'd say, "Here's your mom," and hand the phone to my mom.

I was okay with that because I had written him off and didn't need his approval.

Thirty years after my dad died, during a casual conversation with my sisters, one of them said, "All he talked about was his boy."

I stopped her and said, "What boy?" I thought maybe he was talking about one of his nephews or a grandson.

She said, "He was talking about you, Rockhead! He constantly talked about you to anyone who would listen. He kept a recording of your voice next to his bed. He loved you more than anything in this world!"

I was dumbfounded. Why did everyone know this but me? Why didn't he tell me? He never told me he was proud of me, at least not that I can remember; he never voiced his approval to me; and for the life of me, I don't remember him ever saying "I love you." I thought he had discommended me long ago.

It shook me to my core, and I tried to retrace the years to determine what had happened. Was it his fault for not communicating his love for me? Was it my fault for cutting him off and not breaking through the barriers so many men of his generation had toward expressing affection to their sons?

I think it was an unfortunate combination of the two. If I could turn back the hands of time, I would have allowed him his beliefs even if they didn't mesh with my own. I would have called him more often, and when he asked if I was going to church I would have said, "I'm thinking about it, Dad," or maybe even lied and said, "Yes, I'm going to church," just to get past that barrier and have a conversation with my dad.

I would have told him "I love you" even if he couldn't say it himself and understood this was just the way his generation of dads communicated. Saying "I love you" to their male child was just not something that was done.

All those years wasted! I would have loved to have been able to call and talk with him about things going on in my life, to bounce business ideas off him, or to just have heart-to-heart conversations with my dad like I do with my son.

And I wonder how he must have felt, not being able to communicate with his only son. Did it leave a hole in his heart? A deep feeling of remorse comes over me when I think about how he must have felt. He's gone now, but I hope he knows that I love him, I tell him all the time now.

Don't get me wrong. If you ask my wife Nancy, she'll tell you I still live up to my Rockhead name, and we have managed to raise a son, Taj, who is probably even more hardheaded than I am. He'd argue with me on that, but the apple doesn't fall far from the tree. Both Taj and I have enough sense, though, not to let our hardheaded nature get in the way of our relationship, and neither of us have any problem whatsoever with saying "I love you" and finding ways to show that love.

There are many good things about religion that I admire, and there are many people who use religion to do great things for the world and other people. As long as there are people on this earth, there will be religions, and as long as there are religions, people are going to use them to mimic what is in their hearts.

If they are true givers, and their hearts are full of love, religion will magnify their giving and will become their conduit to the world. These folks give from the goodness of their hearts, and if they were not involved in a religious organization, they would certainly do the same amount of goodness, the same amount of giving. Generally, these people don't feel the need to convert others to their way of thinking; the simple act of giving is their reward. Former president Jimmy Carter, a man I greatly admire, is the ultimate example of this.

There are also the preachers, the shahs, and other religious leaders who, if their intentions are pure, can do a tremendous amount of good for the world. There are others, though, who use the pulpit as an opportunity to further their own agenda under the guise of being a messenger from God. They take sections of the Bible—or the Koran for that matter—and bend it and shape it to their own will. According to World Christian Trends 2001, as of the year 2000, there are over 33,800 denominations in the Christian church, each one having their own twist on Christianity, and sometimes their own interpretation of the Bible.

There are also the followers, some of whom have the external locus of control. If they are involved in a religious organization derived from goodness, and they happen to have a leader who has goodness in his/her heart—well, let's just say I'm glad they have someone who will lead them on a path that does no harm to others and that allows them to join with others in making positive contributions to society.

Religion is a force that can do tremendous good, or it can wreck nations, break cultures, and cause death and destruction. It all depends on who is wielding the book.

***

On one Sunday morning, when I was thirteen years old, while the rest of the family was getting ready for church, I came up with a plan. When it was time to go, I would hide in the closet, and they would have no choice but to go without me. In my mind it was a perfect scheme, and for a while it worked. Of course, like most thirteen-year-old boys, my thought process went as far into the future as the next couple of minutes.

I hid under a pile of clothing in my sister's walk-through closet and listened quietly as they repeatedly called my name.

My mom called, "Ronnie, it's time to go to church."

"Ronnie, we have to go now, or we're going to be late," my dad would add.

Finally, after what seemed like hours, I heard the car doors closing and the car starting, and I finally breathed a sigh of relief as they drove away. I was totally elated; I had done it!

I came out of hiding, ready for some fun! Then it hit me...

They would be returning in a few hours, and my dad was going to be pissed. He would have had a full three hours to build up steam and plan my punishment. By the time he got home, it would have expanded to a royal ass-whooping. The more I thought about it, the more I realized what a mistake I had made.

My plan had been to call Ernest, Beetle, Scooter, and the rest of the guys, hit the streets, and put together a game of basketball or something. But I was so paralyzed with fear that instead of enjoying my respite from church, I never even made it out of the house.

I didn't read—couldn't keep my mind on it. I didn't go out roaming the woods—my legs were too weak from fright. I didn't call my friends for fear they would hear the tremble in my voice. I found myself sitting there trying out different lies:

"I was getting my suit out of my closet when I fainted and fell into a pile of clothing. I didn't wake up until after you guys had left."

"The Lord had sent word directly to me that I was to pray alone at home today."

"I had been abducted by a sect of alien atheists. But don't worry, I was able to escape by quoting Bible verses and holding a cross."

I was never good at lying, especially to my mom. She always knew when I was lying, and all she had to do was to give me that look—you know, "THE LOOK"—and I would fall apart and give a full confession.

So, after careful deliberation, I decided the best option was to come clean, so I just sat on the couch...and waited.

Finally, I heard the car pull up, the doors closing, and *clomp, clomp, clomp*—the footsteps on the porch, the front door opening. The time of reckoning was here!

My sisters filed past one by one, my older sister giving me the "what the fuck were you thinking" look. My little sister had the "you're going to get your ass whooped" smirk.

I was flipping back and forth between coming up with a new and more elaborate lie or coming clean. Then my dad walked in, suit and tie still on, a serious look on his face, and I thought, *Oh, shit, here it comes...*

Then he walked right past me as if nothing had happened.

What the hell had just happened? Was I off the hook? Had he forgotten? Then it dawned on me—I was going to get "THE TALK!"

Chapter 7

STAGES OF DISCIPLINE

I WAS THE ONLY boy of five kids, and I think my parents didn't know what to do with me. I'd get a whooping sometimes, and most times I deserved it. I didn't appreciate it then, but now I'm grateful my dad cared enough to discipline me.

Lots of folks are up in arms now if you as much as smack a kid on the ass, whether they deserve it or not. Then there is the other extreme, where there is absolutely no discipline, and you end up with a young adult who doesn't respect their parents, has no discipline, and later in life finds it hard fitting into society with its necessary rules, laws, and social mores. I believe in being somewhere in the middle.

My discipline came in several levels depending upon the seriousness of my infraction. Level one was my mom and the switch, which basically went like this:

"Go out and cut me a switch because you're going to get a spanking."

Whereupon I would go out to the willow bush and select the wimpiest branch I could find.

It never worked. She would invariably look at it and say, "I said go and get me a switch. Now go back out there and get me a switch!"

So, once again I would venture out to the backyard to select a suitable instrument of my destruction. Then the "spanking" would begin.

My momma was deft on her feet and incredibly accurate with the switch. I would jump, dodge, bob and weave, and run from one corner of the room to the other, but there was no escaping the switch. No matter how fast I moved, the switch seemed to be in the same space in time as my ass. If someone had happened to be walking by and glanced in the window, they would probably say something like, "Damn, Ronnie can get down! I didn't know that dude could dance like that!"

My momma's mantra was "You gonna do it again? You gonna do it again?"

I would yell at the top of my voice, "NO, MOMMA, I'M NOT GONNA DO IT AGAIN!"

But she would continue her target practice. "You gonna do it again? You gonna do it again?"

At some point, when she assumed that I had learned my lesson or her swinging arm just got tired, the spanking would stop. Then she would hug me and tell me how much she loved me and that I needed to do better.

"You can do better than that" was something that stuck with me throughout my life. Even after I grew up and had a family, all my mom had to say was "You can do better than that," and it would bring me back around to reality and snap me out of whatever dumbass thing I was about to do.

Later in my life, when my kids were around three and six years of age—you know, the really "cute" ages, my momma came out to Oregon for a visit. We went out to one of our favorite restaurants for dinner one night, and as we were waiting for our food to arrive, the kids decided to go around to other tables and collect straws. Of course, we thought it was the cutest thing, and assumed everyone else thought the same. We didn't consider they were interrupting conversations and making a nuisance of themselves to people who probably did not appreciate how "cute" they were as much as we did.

Momma sat through the whole dinner without saying a word about it, but on the way out she pulled me aside and whispered to me, *"Ronnie, you can do better than that."*

My knees almost buckled. It was like an electric shock through my system—suddenly, I was a kid again, getting reprimanded for doing something stupid. It snapped me out of it and made me realize that everyone didn't appreciate their actions the way we did. I never let them run around and disturb people like that again. Thanks for the reminder, Momma.

The second level of discipline was "The Whooping," which was usually administered by my dad. It was reserved for especially stupid things—my specialty. Like taking the cake my mom had made for the family, turning it upside down, eating the whole inside, and turning it right side up thinking no one would notice, or putting my fist through the window to get in the house because my sister had locked me out—you know, stupid things like that.

Whooping's went like this: My mom would say, "Go upstairs and wait for your daddy to come home." Well, I don't know if you have ever experienced time standing still, but I did. I'd sit on my bed waiting, waiting...time would slow almost to a standstill for me, knowing what was coming at the end of my wait. By the time my dad got home, I was a mass of quivering protoplasm, unable to speak or move.

My daddy had a butcher strap he kept in his closet just for me. It was a quarter-inch thick and about two inches wide (that's an exaggeration), and he could wield that thing deftly. When I heard him coming up the stairs, I knew he had the butcher strap in his right hand. When he reached the top of the stairs, he'd say, "Bend over," and *SMACK*, the strap would have an intimate connection with my ass. He never really hurt me. The butcher strap was more for intimidation than anything else, but it was enough to make me realize that whatever it was I did wasn't worth this consequence.

The third level, however, was by far the worst, and it sometimes came after the conclusion of the whooping, or he might even skip the whooping and go directly to level three. It was "THE TALK." I realized later in my life that the strap was just to get my attention and make me more receptive for The Talk.

Sometimes he'd start with what seemed like an innocent-sounding conversation like, "How was your day today?" and would go on like that for a while, but just when I was starting to get comfortable, it would take a bad turn. He'd start talking about the consequences of my actions and how there are consequences to everything you do in life, whether they come in the form of the butcher strap administered by himself or some other consequence administered by someone else, and how before every action you take you should be thinking, *What are the consequences of this action?*

Then he would move on to "Your duty to the family, to the church, and to the Lord." And "Our family has a good name in the neighborhood, and we depend on you to represent the family well. You're the only son, and therefore you must carry on the family name." He could go on for what seemed like hours nonstop. By then, I was usually in tears. I would much rather just take the two-minute whooping and get it over with than sit through The Talk.

He would then move on to the question and answer period:

"What were you thinking when you decided to perform this action?"

"How do you think the other person felt about this action?"

"What do you think the consequences should be?"

"What could you have done instead?"

"If this situation comes up again, what are you going to do?"

He would talk about "the Big Mistake," which was the one that could cost someone's life or your own, land you in jail, or have some other major consequence. Every time you are about to do something stupid, you must think, *Is this the Big Mistake?*

I found myself talking with my kids about "the Big Mistake." I'm sure my sisters talked with their kids about the Big Mistake, and their children talked to their kids about the Big Mistake. Fortunately, none of us have ever made the Big Mistake. Of the five children in my family, and the numerous nieces, nephews, grandchildren, and great-grandchildren, none of us ever went to jail, got strung out on drugs, or any of the myriad bad things that were rife in our neighborhood. We all ended up with professional careers in business, education, and politics (as you'll see, though, I took a round-about way to get there). This is remarkable if you look at the rate of incarcerations and number of deaths of young Black folks in Cincinnati from that time to present.

I think after a while my dad realized basically nothing worked with this weird creature that inhabited his house, and whenever I did some asinine thing—which was often—he'd just look at me, shake his head, and walk away.

I would think to myself, *I won.*

Fast-forward twenty years, and I found myself sitting one of my kids down and giving them "THE TALK" and watching them squirm in their seat wishing I would stop. The talks I gave were uncomfortably similar to what my dad had given, *sans* the Bible talk.

Fast-forward another fifteen years, and I got a call from Tonie, my oldest daughter.

"Dad, I am so pissed right now!" she said in a highly agitated voice.

"Why? What's going on, Tonie?" I said, hoping it wasn't something serious.

She replied, "I just caught myself giving one of my kids "THE TALK"—you know, the talk you used to give to me when I was a kid that I hated so much!"

I think my dad won.

No—actually, the world wins because we are all better off. The discipline we take time to give our kids molds them into people who take responsibility for their own actions, people who think before they act, people who are respectful and kind to others.

Seems kind of simple, doesn't it? But just think about it—if all kids got "The Talk," isn't that one of the things that would help move our world in the right direction?

My mother and father knew what they were doing, and it worked. Thank you, Mom and Dad.

Those simple words, "You can do better than that," and "There are consequences to everything you do," always made me stop for a split second whenever I was about to do something stupid—and most times I would fade into the background and let the rest of the gang commit the act of stupidity without me.

The butcher strap and the switch were things my parents used to get my attention, but the talks are what stuck with me.

All three of our children got disciplined in one way or another. Of course, they would try to slide one past you, and sometimes you just have to let it go. They do need to be able to get away with some things; otherwise they will feel as if they have no power, and it's important for them to feel empowered because their own sense of empowerment is what is going to sustain them when they leave your nest and go out into the world.

***

All of our kids had chores they had to do every week. Their chores were not connected to an allowance or anything like that. It was understood that the chores were their contribution to keeping the family and household functioning.

One Saturday evening when Jazmin, my second daughter, was sixteen and had her own car, she was preparing to go out to a party with friends. I watched her get dressed, put on her makeup—spending time in front of the mirror to make sure she was looking good. By the time she was done she was looking good and ready to party.

I waited until she was about to step out the door, stopped her, and said, "Are you going to weed the yard dressed like that?"

She got that stricken "oh, shit" look we sometimes see on people's faces when they know they are wrong and there's no way out. Of course, she hadn't forgotten about the weeding, she just thought she could slide one past me.

The next day my neighbor Marvin called and said, "Hey, Ron, what was Jazmin doing out in the yard with her car headlights on in the middle of the night? Did she lose something?" When I told him, he busted out laughing because he had pretty much done the same thing with one of his boys.

I agree: it was harsh, but she never forgot the lesson. She is probably one of the most conscientious people I know. She called me when she was twenty-seven and said, "Dad, thank you so much for disciplining us. I see the results of no discipline in some of the kids I work with now, and it's really sad!"

I disciplined my kids' friends, too. I told them, "The first couple of times you come to our house, you're a guest, but after that, you are one of my kids, and you are expected to eat everything on your plate, clean up after yourself, and do all of the other things my kids know to do."

I taught the kids that, when an adult addresses you, shake their hand firmly, look them in the eye, and answer in a strong voice. Open the door for a lady and let her go first, and don't chew with your mouth open! If they accepted something, however trivial, and didn't say thanks, I'd say, "What? I didn't hear you!" Those two words, "thank you," are the magic keys that will open many doors.

It didn't take them long to get it.

Later in life, as an owner of several businesses, I sometimes ended up being the "dad" to lots of grown-up kids in my employ; teaching them the concepts of consequences, responsibility, manners, and many of the social mores' parents need to teach their kids to equip them to function well in our society. Unfortunately, their parents had not taken the time, so, as a result, many of them were clueless about how to conduct themselves in the world. I've had more than a few of them come back later and thank me for the lessons.

It takes a lot of strength and fortitude to be a good parent. It's easy to say, "It's okay; they will learn somehow" and shirk the responsibilities of parenthood. But, if you bring them into the world, you need to accept that responsibility and do the right thing by them. That is pretty much all you owe them.

You don't owe them a college education; they can pay for that themselves if you raise them right—and they will really appreciate their education when they've paid for part of it. You don't owe them a car; by the time they're old enough to drive they should have worked long enough to buy their own car. You don't even owe them an inheritance because by the time you die, they should be standing on their own feet and shouldn't need your money.

Conversely, they don't owe you anything except to grow up and be responsible contributors to society—that's it.

***

Kids can be challenging sometimes. Hopefully they are smarter than us, though, and that's what you should want. They can outwit us and cause us angst, but someone must be the adult, and if we don't play the role of adult and do the listening and teaching that comes along with being the parent, at some point it's too late. When they leave home, instead of thanking you for disciplining them, they will wonder, "Why didn't my parents teach me about this?" and then someone or some institution will have to educate them on things their parents should have taught them.

Unfortunately, single-parent homes have become too common in Black American families, and many times it is the dad who is absent. This can create double duty for single moms. Mothers in the Black community are traditionally be the pillars of strength. There is a level of strength in Black women that has withstood centuries of tribulations, but they keep doing a great job of raising our Black youth. Sometimes, though, they may need a little help. I encourage Black men to take part in the raising of their own families. You took part in breeding, so you should shoulder some of the responsibility of raising your kids. Don't breed them if you can't feed them, and that goes for mind, body and spirit.

If you don't have kids of your own, and you see a young man or woman struggling, they may be at a turning point in their life. Help them out. Lend a helping hand, be a good listener, offer a word of advice or encouragement when appropriate. Plant a seed that could help them to turn in the right direction. That same kid could be robbing you on the street someday if you don't.

There are many organizations that identify kids needing mentors, but you don't necessarily need to go through one of these organizations. Look around your neighborhood. That kid down the street who is just hanging out with nothing to do? Give him something to do. The young lady who just doesn't seem to fit in? Try to find out what she is interested in and help her connect with like-minded kids. They'll probably look at you like you are the dumbest thing on earth, which is pretty much what they have to do—it's in their teenage genes. But don't think they aren't listening or that what you say doesn't affect them. You may not see the fruition of the seeds you plant, but the words you say and the attention you give may change a life.

Looking back, I certainly didn't appreciate the discipline my parents dished out at the time, but now I am so glad my parents were strong enough to persist and give me the foundations on which to build. It took a long time for their lessons to make their way through my thick skull, but eventually they did—and I was able to pass them along to my children.

Thank you, Mom and Dad, for being strong.

Chapter 8

PLANTING SEEDS

R ECENTLY, I WAS IN line at one of our local hardware stores when the young lady at the cash register, after looking at my driver's license, asked, "Are you Jazmin's dad?"

I said, "Why, yes, I am. Why? Do you know her?"

She answered, "When I was in grade school, Jazmin took time out of her busy schedule to teach a dance class for me and some of my friends. I still remember how good we felt that this high school senior took the time to help us little grade-school kids out." She continued with a teary look in her eyes, "She made us feel important, and it totally helped me with my self-esteem at a difficult time in my life."

When I told Jazmin about it, she got a little smile on her face and said, "It was as much fun for me as it was for them, but I had no idea it had affected them that much."

That was a seed that had been planted that obviously had a positive effect on these young girl's lives, and Jazmin never would have known it if that young lady hadn't noticed the last name on my driver's license.

With the dishonest and misogynistic messages our forty-fifth president and others in the limelight have put forth, we really need positive role models to let young people know this is not the norm. "We can do better than that." I am convinced there are more honest, ethically minded people in this world than there are bad. There are a countless number of good deeds taking place in our country and in the world every day; it's just that the good deeds aren't newsworthy, so you never hear about them.

In an interview on MTV, Barack Obama stated, "Brothers should pull up their pants. You're walking by your mother, your grandmother, and your underwear is showing. What's wrong with that? Come on. There are some issues that we face that you don't have to pass a law about, but that doesn't mean folks can't have some sense and some respect for other people and, you know, some people might not want to see your underwear—I'm one of them."

We may not want to admit it, but the world judges you largely by the way you present yourself; if you dress like a thug, people are going to assume you are a thug—so don't expect them to hire you to represent them in public. If you dress for success, generally you are on your way to success, and you should consider yourself successful for even taking that step.

As an employer I was amazed at the attire people would show up in for an interview. I know this is generalizing and being judgmental, but I assume if you dress sloppy, you'll do sloppy work, so unless you are a genius or something, and I can see past your exterior, chances are I'm not going to hire you to do anything of importance.

The same goes for your manner of speech. If you want to work in mainstream America and make mainstream bucks, your chances are better if you take the time to learn the mainstream dialect. Your chances are much better at obtaining meaningful employment or making changes in a country whose mainstream language is standard English if you speak standard English. I'm not saying that you have to—that's a choice you need to make.

Chapter 9

UNDER THE BRIDGE

W E SAT IN THE car with the engine running. It was a cold night, but it seemed even colder under the bridge where we sat. The mist drifting up from the river sucked any color out of the air, making everything seem black, white, and shades of gray and adding to the eeriness of the night. A light rain fell, giving a soft luster to the asphalt. Under the bridge where we sat, it was dry.

Except for Chris, we were all too young to go into the bar that was tucked between the bridge pilings. It was a small bar with dark, ominous windows, located across the river in Covington, Kentucky. No light going in or coming out, just one solitary light over the maroon red door—this was the only color in the night. We were waiting for Chris to come out. We had stopped there because he needed to meet someone to do some business. Sometimes you didn't ask questions about other people's business. We didn't have anything else to do that night but hang out, anyway, and this was as good a place as any.

The door of the bar opened as two obviously drunk men came tumbling out of the bar. The fight had started inside but was forced outside because of the bar owner's need to keep things orderly. They tussled for a while, then backed off from each other like two rams building up steam for another charge.

Suddenly we heard a loud *pop, pop, pop.* I never saw the pistol, just heard the pops, and then the shooter took off into the night, disappearing into the darkness.

The second guy fell to the ground, his head cocked at a weird angle against a car parked in front, dark liquid oozing from a wound in his chest. I started the windshield wipers, and we sat there for a minute, watching to see if he was going to move again. He began the dead man twitch we'd all seen before...and then he stopped. His body relaxed, and his head slid sideways along the tire, bumped off the fender, and came to rest under the tire. We knew he wasn't getting up again.

Patrons came creeping out of the bar to see what the commotion was. When they saw him lying there, one by one they slunk away, disappearing like wraiths into the misty night. Nobody wanted to be a witness.

Chris came out of the bar, stepped over the dead man's legs, and crossed the street to the car. I started the car and did a U-turn to head back over the bridge from Covington to Cincinnati. Chris said from the back seat, "Hey, man, thanks for waiting. Where do ya'll wanna go now?"

By the time I was sixteen, I had seen five people killed. Four of these killings were a Black man killing another Black man, and the fifth was a Black man killing a Black woman. This past Memorial Day, I opened the morning paper to read that there had been fifty-two people shot and ten killed in Chicago that weekend. The paper went on to say this was a drastic drop from past Memorial Days. Most of these deaths were Black men killing other Black men.

Last time I was back visiting in Cincinnati, I got together with some friends from the old neighborhood—the ones who were left. After reminiscing about the hood, talk turned to old friends. We talked about a friend who had been beaten to death by another Black man and another who had been shot. I remembered why I had stopped asking about old friends in the neighborhood; I was tired of hearing about people dying or going to jail. What the hell is wrong with us, that we continue to kill each other off at such an alarming rate?

Years later, sitting in a sociology class while studying at the University of Oregon, we were looking at a map of Los Angeles and the associated violent crimes for each neighborhood, with a red dot representing each violent crime. In the more affluent White sections of Los Angeles there were no red dots; in the Hispanic neighborhoods, dots were scattered here and there; but when we got to the Black sections of town, it was almost solid red, like they had run out of room for dots. The red dots in the Black neighborhoods did not signify bank robberies or white-collar crimes—nothing like that; ninety percent of those red dots were Black people doing bad things to other Black people.

I was the only Black person in the class, and I sat there embarrassed. I knew I wasn't involved, but I couldn't help but wonder what it is about us that causes Black folks to go about killing each other with such gusto.

I have thought through some potential causes: Is it tribal? Are we still operating on the old tribal warfare model that we still see in parts of Africa: Hutu vs. Tutsi, Sudan's Nuer, and Dinka? There's really no need for it here in the United States, though; most of us have no idea what part of Africa our ancestors were from—much less which tribe.

In so many instances we have become our own worst enemy.

I know lots of Black folks want to blame everything on the White man, much like some unemployed Whites of lower socioeconomic status like to blame everything on Jews, Blacks, and liberals. This takes me back to something I remember learning in college.

There's a psychology concept called the "locus of control" that says there are two different mentalities: internal locus of control and external locus of control.

People with an external locus of control believe their destiny is controlled by some external force, be it the government, Jews, Blacks, Whites, the liberal press, FOX News, Jesus, God...see where I'm going? The thing about the external locus of control mentality is that you basically never have to accept responsibility for your actions or position, since it's never your fault, and you can never run out of people, organizations, or entities to blame. As long as you have that list of others or external forces, you don't have to take responsibility for your actions or lack of action.

Sometimes I am envious of people who can buy into this concept. I mean, just think:

Can't get a job? It's the Mexicans' fault for taking all the jobs.

Don't have enough money? Must be the fault of the Jews; they have all the money.

Do something bad? The devil made me do it!

No matter what the deed, it's always okay, and you don't have to take responsibility for it because it's out of your control. What a wonderful thing—if you can accept that!

The upside of this locus for you, then (and downside for everyone else), is, since your plight is not your fault, and you don't have to take responsibility, you can sit back and blame it on the group or entity of choice and just stay right where you are. After all, there's nothing you can do about it anyway, so why even try?

Internal locus of control folks believe their good fortunes, as well as their downfalls, are a result of their actions or lack thereof. If they screw up, they take responsibility and take steps to correct the action and make sure it doesn't happen again. If they are successful, they don't call it luck or the will of God; they take credit for their accomplishments. Sure, to appear humble they may give credit to someone else or some entity or call it luck. But deep inside, they know their station in life is largely due to their actions or inaction.

There are loads of psychological, physical, economic, and emotional barriers African Americans have to deal with in this country; systemic racism and economic disparities, just for a start. As long as we accept that things are out of our control, we will stay under the knee. We must take steps to overcome these barriers in whatever way we can. Some do, some don't; but if you are on that path, consider yourself successful. A culture that teaches a lack of control fosters inaction, sometimes leading to learned helplessness. This is what we must work against because, once a child has been indoctrinated into this way of thinking, it takes a tremendous amount of work to turn him or her around. This may be the first step in learning how to work together to achieve some semblance of equality.

I am inspired by the recent continuation of the equal rights movement taking place in this country and the awakening happening as a result. I'm also encouraged by the fact that so many Black and multiracial young folk are leading the way. For centuries we had little, if any, control over our destinies, and now we have the opportunity to face and overcome the barriers that have kept us down for so long. I'm not saying it's going to be easy; there are so many people in power who will try to sabotage us at every step. We are going to have many failures for every success because the oligarchs have convinced themselves that keeping us down is the key to their success. But like the Temptations' song "Message from a Black Man" says, "*No matter how hard you try, you can't stop me now.*"

***

Minorities in this country still have massive barriers confronting them. Many of these obstacles have been removed or at least softened by the giants who came before us: people like Rosa Parks, Fredrick Douglass, Barack and Michelle Obama, and countless numbers of Black, White, Asian, gay, and Jewish folks who marched in the streets, getting chased by dogs, beaten, and washed down the street with fire hoses—all so we could have opportunities, simple things like voting, getting the education denied to us for so long, and owning property. As long as we fall back on excuses—of which there are many—and use them to keep us from moving forward, we will continue to wallow in our own sorrow and stay where we are. We need to acknowledge we are starting from a huge deficit and work to overcome the deficit. And when you reach a point where you feel you have made it, reach over and show someone else how to climb the ladder—be a mentor.

***

"There is a lack of interest in voting in the United States, and that troubles me. It is very necessary that people get registered, study the issues and be aware of the politics of our country. We will really be set back if people don't take the time to learn about the candidates who are concerned about the wellbeing of all the citizens and vote."

———**Rosa Parks**

So many people have fought and died for the opportunity to have a voice in defining our destiny. If you choose not to vote, all their efforts are for naught.

After the election of the forty-fifth president of the United States, I saw an interview that took place in one of our inner cities. It was at an all-Black barbershop, and the reporter interviewing the group was listening to the bitching and moaning going on about the forty-fifth presidential administration. She then asked how many people in the shop had voted. Sixty-five percent of them had not voted, yet they had the audacity to complain about the outcome of the election!

This is another one of those moments that makes you scratch your head in amazement. In my opinion, if you're able to vote and choose not to, you lose the right to complain about the outcome. You had a chance to make a difference, and you chose not to use it. Notice I said you "chose" not to use it. It was a choice you made, and a poor choice at that. Sometimes there are barriers put in place to try and prevent you from voting, but you need to find ways to overcome these barriers, or at least make the effort, and vote for politicians who will eliminate the barriers. Vote in national elections, but also vote in your local elections because these are the elections that will affect your school systems and local laws that will influence everyday life for you and your family.

I know some Black Americans say, "Why should I vote? My vote is not going to make any difference!" Well, the other side voted, and guess what? It made a difference for them—they won!

***

I had a conversation with my daughter about her consternation that one of her White friends didn't know anything about the issues of being Black in America, which led to a discussion of the apathy and lack of concern for minorities by many Whites living in Middle America.

I asked, "Why would they care? I know they should, but why would they?"

They go to work every day and deal with like-minded people, are in communities sharing the same values and outlooks, and listen to FOX or Newsmax programs that share their same political views. Then they come home to their comfortable homes in those same like-minded communities.

As far as they are concerned, their world is perfect, so why muddle things by digging into other people's problems and concerns? They are in that euphoric state known as White privilege, and they don't even know it. It's as natural to them as breathing.

Unless something catastrophic happens that pushes them out of their cocoon of comfort, or they happen to come in contact with someone who leads in a way that enables them to begin to see the other side, they will likely live their whole life happily in their never-neverland and go to their deaths none the wiser. This is not to absolve them of the offense of indifference; the information is there if they choose to access it, but for reasons of convenience, they have chosen to ignore it. If you asked them, they would swear they were not racist; some people would say that the very fact that they don't take the simple steps to become informed about issues affecting minorities in this country is a form of racism.

I reminded my daughter that she was fortunate enough to have been raised in a family bridging both extremes of the racial and economic spectrum; her mom a White person from Dearborn, Michigan, which was once described as the last bastion of White supremacy; and her dad, a Black man from Cincinnati, Ohio, a place at the end of the Mason-Dixie line, a place that is forty-five percent Black and consistently quoted as one of the five most racist cities in the country. She had no choice but to see both sides because she is a living, breathing product of these two opposite ends of the spectrum.

The adage "Walk a mile in my shoes" is almost impossible for some in this respect. I can't expect a White person to completely understand what it's like being Black, and I don't know what it's like to be White. But you don't have to completely understand another's "all" in order to have empathy. To be clear, I don't want sympathy. What I want is a level playing field, and for the oligarchs and their enforcers, ie. GOP and police to get their knees off of our necks and quit blocking our efforts to achieve equal footing. Simple things like equal access to education for Black children, programs to help Black families overcome the disparity in wealth and ownership of real estate and police reform to name a few.

***

"Race doesn't really exist for you because it has never been a barrier. Black folks don't have that choice." ——**Chimamanda Ngozi Adichie**

We've come a long way from the days of public hangings, but our young Black men are still being shot and killed by the very people who are sworn to protect them—with no recourse. Our voting rights are constantly being challenged through redistricting, voter ID requirements, and whatever other impediments some in the GOP can dream up. We still have a long way to go to gain equal access to education for our inner-city youth. We have come a long way, but we still have a long way to go, and the threat of slipping backwards is always there. The consequences are far too great for us to rest on our laurels.

Every one of us is an emissary of our race whether we want to be or not. Every contact you have with anyone, no matter what race, country, or religion they are, has an impact on how we move forward as we exist in this world together. The words you say and the things you do carry more weight than what people read in the newspaper or see on TV. This holds true for Black people, White people, Hispanics—everyone.

In a perfect world we could say, "Don't judge a whole race by my actions." But in so many cases, that's the only thing some folks have to go on, so the easiest thing to do is to treat everyone with respect whether you feel they deserve it or not. Remember, you aren't doing it for them. You are doing it for your own dignity, your family and for all of us. If given a choice—and there's always a choice—take the high road.

Chapter 10

CATCH THE FIRST THING SMOKIN'

VIOLENCE BETWEEN RACES WAS thick in Cincinnati back in the '60s and still is. Talking to my mom one day, long after I had left Cincy, I asked about one of my friends, Gary. She explained to me that Gary had been driving through Norwood and had gotten into a racially tinged argument over the CB radio. He had agreed to meet the other guy in a supermarket parking lot to settle their differences. My mom said, "Gary didn't even get a chance to go for his gun. They found it on the seat beside him after the guy shot him."

I thought, *What the hell is this, the Wild, Wild West or something?* And it brought back to me why I had left Cincy and never went back. Don't get me wrong; I had a great childhood growing up in Cincinnati. I would not trade my childhood there for anything in the world. I loved living in the city; we never ran out of things to do.

At some point, though, things got too serious for me, or maybe I just realized the consequences of staying.

I wasn't like some of the guys I knew. Some of them had nothing to lose, and they would just as soon kick your ass as look at you. Many of them had what amounted to "timeshare cells" in jail or juvi. They would get out of jail, somebody would piss them off, and "pop," someone would be dead—and back to jail they went. It was like going home for these guys; their cell was their equivalent of a condo.

Although I hung with these guys, I realized early on that I wasn't like them. I wasn't a badass; I never picked a fight with anyone. Any fight I had was instigated by the other party and a result of me defending myself or someone else.

My final exodus from Cincinnati was prompted by an incident I was lucky to have escaped from with my life. I had broken up with my longtime girl and was seeing a different girl out in Lincoln Heights, an area outside of Cincinnati proper that included a series of housing projects that stretched for miles. We used to joke that the Lincoln Heights dudes just ate raw meat and beans because they were like gorillas: big, strong, and ugly.

One night, my friend R.D. and I were leaving Lincoln Heights when a car pulled up next to us. The driver was revving his engine, and I knew something was up. I was riding shotgun, and I looked over and right into the barrel of a gun—a gun with a barrel that looked big enough to fit a baseball. Then, from the back of the car I heard, "Get yo ass out of Lincoln Heights, and don't come back!"

I didn't have to tell R.D. to go. He hit the gas, running the stoplight. We hit the freeway doing ninety and headed back to our neighborhood.

Anyone in their right mind would have just left and not gone back, right? Not us. We gathered about six carloads of dudes from my neighborhood, Avondale, and downtown and went back. I was supposed to take on the leader of the Lincoln Heights gang to start it off, which caused more than a little anxiety for me as I had no idea who this guy was or how big he was.

We drove around for a while, piled out of the cars, and walked the streets a bit. Lucky for me, we couldn't find anyone, so we left Lincoln Heights and went back home.

But we had awakened a sleeping giant. No one ever messed with Lincoln Heights, and we found out why. The Lincoln Heights gang got word of what we had done and started retaliating. They started coming to the neighborhood and just kicking ass, walking down the street in the middle of day and basically sweeping the neighborhood.

Word was, when they caught me, I would be dead—and I believed them. So, I did the only sensible thing: I joined the Army! I know, I know; that makes no sense at all, especially since this was 1966 and we were in the thick of the Vietnam War, right when the Tet Offensive was happening.

I joined the Army, not because I was anxious to go to war, but because even with the Vietnam War going on, I felt my odds were better in the Army than on the streets of Cincinnati.

When I left, I sold my car to my sister. It was a beautiful baby blue 1958 Ford Galaxy with a white convertible top, white roll-and-tuck seats, and dual exhaust with glass packs on both sides. It had a 352-cubic-inch interceptor engine and had been clocked at close to ninety-eight miles per hour on the freeway, and that was after I had slowed down. I know because it said so on the ticket I got from the state trooper.

I should have warned my sister not to take it out to Lincoln Heights. She did, though, and came out of a party one night to find the car surrounded by a bunch of big, ugly Lincoln Heights gorillas asking, "Is this Ronnie Tinsley's car?" My sister feigned ignorance and said, "Ronnie who?" Luckily, they left her alone.

Leaving Cincinnati was a turning point in my life. Years later, while visiting me in Hawaii, my mom remarked, "I really miss having you around, but I'm sure glad you left Cincinnati." Unsaid was her fear that if I had stayed in Cincy, I would have ended up dead or in jail.

She later confided in me that when I was late coming home or didn't come home at night her first three calls were; first—to my friends to see if I was there, second—to the police to see if they had me, and third—to the hospitals to see if I was there.

Sorry Momma.

Chapter 11

ARMY DAYS, 1966

I WAS TOTALLY UNPREPARED for my first night at Fort Knox, Kentucky. I remember standing outside in the freezing rain shivering in only a lightweight trench coat while a big, burly staff sergeant stood on a covered deck yelling at us, telling us what lowlife maggots we were and how he was going to be our mother, father, preacher, and teacher. We had no choice but to stand there shivering in the freezing rain, listening to him go on and on. It was the shape of things to come.

In military training, they start the process of breaking you down as soon as you hit boot camp. For some people it may be the only discipline they receive in their lives. I feel like it's a good thing for young men to have to go through (if it wasn't for going to war) because it's the closest thing to initiation rites many young men and women have besides gangs. The military teaches responsibility, consequences, and discipline. It will also either get you in shape or kick your ass, or a little of both.

Most societies have some form of initiation or rites of passage young people go through to reach adulthood. These serve to teach them the rules and social mores and help them clarify their position in society.

"Initiation rites are seen as fundamental to human growth and development as well as socialization in many African communities. These rites function by ritually marking the transition of someone to full group membership. It also links individuals to the community and the community to the broader and more potent spiritual world. Initiation rites are 'a natural and necessary part of a community, just as arms and legs are natural and necessary extension of the human body.' These rites are linked to individual and community development."

——**Wikipedia**

There is also a certain comradery you get when you overcome physical and mental obstacles in the company of others. It's the kind of comradery that can last a lifetime.

I enjoyed basic training once I got into it. I even learned to like the sergeant I had hated so much that first day. I saw him in Louisville one night and had a couple of drinks with him. I found out he was actually a pretty good guy—just doing his job.

Basic training was hard on some guys. Some broke down mentally, some broke down physically, and some just broke. One night I heard a commotion in the bay and stepped out to see what was going on. Standing there in the middle of the room was a guy who had been having a hard time adjusting to being away from home, army life, and the prospect of going to war. He had slit both wrists and was standing there bleeding out. We got the medics to him quickly, and hopefully he made it. I never heard what happened to him after that.

I had signed up for reconnaissance and went through the armored recon training at Fort Knox. These are the folks out front in small, agile track vehicles (tanks), which we called rolling coffins because, although they might stop a bullet, an artillery shell or land mine would blow them and everyone in them all to hell. I was scheduled to attend Officer Candidate School to become a second lieutenant—and then it was on to Vietnam. One day, one of the older brothers who had just come back from Nam pulled me aside and said, "Hey, man, you better back out of that officer shit, cause if the Cong don't kill you, your own men will." I found out later what the life expectancy of a recon second lieutenant in Nam was and decided to change my military occupation code to military police.

Which took me to Fort Gordon, Georgia.

Chapter 12

THE DEEP SOUTH

"*I*F YOU CAN CONVINCE *the lowest white man he's better than the best colored man, he won't notice you're picking his pocket. Hell, give him somebody to look down on, and he'll empty his pockets for you.*"

————**Lyndon B. Johnson**

Fort Gordon, Georgia, was my first introduction to the Deep South. It was the training camp for the military police academy and advanced airborne infantry training. Suffocatingly hot, Fort Gordon was dusty and full of snakes, some with no legs and some with two. The kind of place that once you've been there, you never want to go back.

I was the only Black person in my company of 150 men. I knew I was in for an interesting time when, while standing in line in the mess hall, someone walked by and whispered, "You know what we do to people like you down here, don't you?"

"Huh???"

My first night in the barracks was a sleepless one. When the lights went out someone yelled, "We gonna hang us a nigger tonight." I assumed they were talking about me because I was the only Black person in the building. There were others who joined in that night, talking about what they do to niggers in the South, using some pretty descriptive adjectives. I even got called a nigger while in formation on the parade grounds. Nothing was said about it, nothing was done about it—it was just accepted behavior in the South during that time, even in the military.

Well, I knew I couldn't fight them all, and I knew our sergeant was a racist asshole, so going to him was out of the question. So, I slept with a knife with me every night, not knowing if or when I was going to be dragged outside and beaten—or worse. I spent a lot of sleepless nights at Fort Gordon. It's an experience I don't care to relive.

There was another Black guy in another company who I got to know. What he described in his barracks pretty much mirrored what I went through.

When you stepped off base from Fort Gordon into Augusta, Georgia, you were entering the Old South, replete with Confederate flags and other reminders of your position in society if you were anything other than White. In 1966 they were still hanging Black men for looking too hard at White women—and this wasn't long after Emmitt Till. There had been over four hundred documented lynchings in Georgia by that time in history, only exceeded by Mississippi's toll of five hundred plus. These numbers didn't include the backwoods lynchings that were never reported. Needless to say, this created some tension for Black American troops.

I was in Fort Gordon for 8-weeks, which seemed like an eternity for me. I was glad to be done with it—and with the Deep South. It took me another forty years before I returned to the South, and that was only because my daughter Tonie lived there at the time.

Just this little taste of the South gave me a better understanding of why my dad left there, never went back, and would not even talk about it. The Great Migration of Blacks from the South was made up of people trying to escape situations far worse than mine. For them, the threat of hanging was not just a threat; it was a real part of their everyday life.

Sitting around, listening to some of the older folks who had come north from the South, I remember them saying, "If you go out in the woods, you might run into some 'strange fruit.'" For years I didn't know what they meant by "strange fruit." I thought it was some poisonous vine or something. Years later I was listening to a Billie Holiday song by the same name and did some investigating. I found out that "strange fruit" was another name for Black folks hanging from trees—an all-too-common sight in the South at the time. She wrote the song because during one of her tours, because she wasn't allowed to use White bathrooms, and there were no others available, she got off the bus to go to the bathroom in the woods and looked up to see a Black man hanging from a tree—just left there hanging, with wind blowing his tattered clothes and crows picking at his rotting flesh.

If you wonder why you don't see many Black folks out backpacking in the woods, this is probably why. For centuries, if White men caught a lone Black man, woman, or child in the woods, they felt like they could do anything they wanted to them without fear of recrimination. Even to this day I feel if it's my word against a White dude, I'm going to get the worst of it while he is going to get the benefit of doubt.

***

After eight long weeks at Fort Gordon I shipped out to my permanent base, Fort Shafter, Hawaii, arriving at around one o'clock in the morning with my duffle bag over my shoulder. While walking down the hallway on the way to my bunk I slipped on something. Looking down I realized it was blood—on the floor, on the walls, and on a really pissed-off-looking dude sitting on the stairs flicking a knife and talking about "Killing some motherfucker." He didn't look at me or even acknowledge me, so I stepped around him and went up to find my bunk. I don't know what had gone down that night, but it didn't involve me, and I never found out.

There was a lot of tension in the air, partly from soldiers coming back from Nam, fighting a war they didn't understand, being told to kill little brown men and women because some politician told them they were fighting for our freedom—and then slowly coming to the realization of what they had done. Contrary to what you see Rambo or John Wick do on screen, most people don't walk away from killing someone without having it change them forever in some way. Someday, somehow, it will come back and inject itself into their dreams and become a part of them, a part that as much as they would like to shake, they can't. And if killing someone doesn't affect you in some way, there's something wired wrong inside your head.

Some soldiers were suffering from PTSD, shell-shock, a guilty conscience—whatever you want to call it. That's the result of young, clueless teenagers going into battle against veteran fighters, seeing things they can't forget, doing things they wish they hadn't, and having to live with the memory and guilt. And for others, there was the palpable fear that the order to ship out to Nam could come at any time.

Young Black soldiers also had to face the fact that, even after putting their lives on the line for this country, for the "freedom" of our democracy, they were still niggers and second-class citizens in the eyes of many when they got back to the U.S.

After being at Fort Shafter for a while, I met a White guy from Arkansas named Sammy Teague. Sammy was a sixth-generation red-neck from Arkansas, a tall, lanky, redhead dude with a chip on his shoulder and an attitude that only a White dude from the South can have. Like many people from that area, he didn't have much use for Black folks. His attitude was that White men had authority over every living thing; racism was as natural to him as it is for squirrels to crack nuts.

I don't know how it happened. Maybe it was because we were in the same place at the same time, or maybe because we shared a love for Southern Comfort, but we slowly began an unlikely friendship. It started with casual conversations while on duty as military police. When you're stuck in a patrol car together for eight hours, it's hard to avoid getting to know each other at least a little. It evolved into us going out on the town together, starting the night with a pint of Southern Comfort, after which you tend to love everybody.

One night we came back to the barracks drunk out of our minds. I made it to my bunk and was about to pass out when I heard someone yelling from the latrine, "Goddamn niggers, niggers! I hate niggers! Niggers can go to hell!"

I realized it was Sammy. I rushed into the latrine, grabbed him, and forcefully took him outside before he woke some of the brothers in the barracks; they probably would have messed him up, and I'd have had a hell of a time stopping them.

After some talking, some threatening, and having to wrestle him to the ground, I was able to get him calmed down. I began trying to get to the root of what was happening. He finally opened up to me and said, "Man, I was raised to believe that you people were the scum of the Earth. I've hated Black people all my life. If I accept you as a friend, I'm going against everything my family believes in. But I love you like a brother, man. What am I supposed to do?"

Then Sammy broke down sobbing—he really didn't know what to do. It was a big deal for him and it was a quandary he was going to have to deal with.

I was able to get Sammy to his bunk that night without further incident. The next day we went out to the bleachers and sat where we wouldn't be interrupted and talked. We talked about the South and his upbringing there. We talked about White attitudes toward Blacks; we talked about the source of his beliefs and what was truth and what were lies; we talked about Black attitudes towards Whites and the source for those beliefs. We were able to begin the awakening process for him.

Sammy had been raised in a community and family that believed Black folks were one step above monkeys: subhuman and not to be trusted. This belief had been passed down through the generations in his family and in his community. It had never been questioned and in time had become fact. It was a common scenario, not only in the South, but also in many other parts of the country. If these beliefs were not challenged, after generations they were eventually just accepted as truth. Over time, the community established a library of misinformation supporting these supposed "truths." They could even pick specific portions of the Bible that, taken out of context, could mean something totally different than the intended message. They took as fact experiences of their ancestors, passed down through generations whether they were true or not. They drew on purveyors of misinformation who were experts at picking out little bits of truth and manipulating them to prove their point.

Sammy had been exposed to someone who didn't fit the description of Black folks he had been led to accept, and once you find one exception— you begin to question the whole truth. A crack had opened in his consciousness that had to be closed off again, or he was going to have to do some serious readjustments. It's hard, gut-wrenching work to reexamine your life and your beliefs and challenge your family, friends, and the whole culture that you've grown up within.

For most people in this situation, it's simplest to think of the exception as an anomaly and just ignore it and go on with their old racist beliefs—it's easier that way.

Over the next few weeks, I had more hard conversations with Sammy. It was much like doing an intervention to cure someone of alcoholism or a long-term addiction. There was always the possibility he was going to slip back to his old norm—and he sometimes did. It was a difficult process for both of us, but Sammy was a good man and, by this time, my friend.

We kept in touch after he was discharged. He stayed in Hawaii and eventually married a beautiful Samoan lady. One day he dropped by the post to see me. I could tell he had something on his mind that was troubling him. I kept trying to pull it out of him until he finally said to me, "I'm going to take my new wife home to Arkansas to meet my family. What do you think?"

I turned to him and said, "Sammy, are they aware of her race? You know they're going to look at her as a Black person, and you know how they feel about Black folks back where you come from."

He said resolutely, "They're going to have to accept her because she's my wife."

He went to Arkansas and was back within a week. He hadn't realized how deep-seated the racism was in the South, in his family, and in his sphere of friends. It even transcended family; they just could not accept her—or him anymore, for that matter. In their minds, he had gone to the dark side and in this case mud was thicker than blood.

We knew, though, that instead of going to the dark side, he had seen the light and could no longer accept the real "dark side," which was the ugly systemic racism that he had been raised with.

Chapter 13

BLOODLUST

O NE OF MY DUTIES as a military police officer was to transport prisoners coming back from Vietnam who were either headed for the brig or to Tripler Army Hospital's mental ward. These were soldiers who had committed crimes like "fragging" their platoon leader or putting a bullet into another GI they had a beef with during a firefight, or who had gotten the "bloodlust" and began to enjoy killing a little too much, which is why many of them went back for two or three tours. It was the only place they could kill people and get away with it. This happened all too often, and it was something us GIs all knew—but you'd never read about it in the paper.

These soldiers with the bloodlust were scary creatures, and I mean "creatures" in the true sense of the word. It seemed as if they had lost whatever it is that made them human and had reverted to something else. They were operating from their hindbrain or medulla—the most primitive part of the brain.

There were some who had gotten so out of hand that the military had no choice but to deal with them, which meant a trip back to the USA and the brig or the mental ward. My job was to meet them and their escort at the Air Force Base, make the exchange, put them in cuffs, and get them into the back seat of my patrol car for transport to the hospital. Even though they were handcuffed with an impenetrable barrier between us, they still made my skin crawl! Most of them had an animalistic look in their eyes, like a caged wildcat, as if they were looking for a weakness or an opportunity to strike.

One of these guys (not one of my charges), a big, slack-jawed, rawboned, country-looking dude with arms that hung down to his knees, somehow got loose and grabbed hold of the major in charge. He had superhuman strength, the kind of raw strength you would expect from a gorilla or some other wild animal. Eyes popping out of his head, grunting, grabbing, he was intent on doing as much damage as possible while he had the major in his grasp.

It took a shitload of guys to extract the major from his grip and get this soldier locked into a treatment room—a room that was about ten by twenty feet with high ceilings. He succeeded in fogging up every window in the room, chest heaving, making weird animal noises. It was a spectacle that still lives in my mind no matter how much I would like to purge it. The incident must have affected the major as well because he left the unit soon after, and we never saw him again. I know he was a trembling mess by the time we got that guy off him.

This is what this war was doing to these young men; maybe they were normal when they left for the war, but many of them had deep psychological scars when they came back. They came back to their loved ones as different, sometimes unrecognizable people; some relationships didn't withstand the changes, and many of these young men ended up on the streets as part of our "homeless problem."

We sent them there—something we shouldn't have done in the first place—and we should have taken care of them when they got back.

Chapter 14

THE RACE THING AGAIN--1967

An insult only has power if you acknowledge it.

D URING THE '60S AND '70S there were two different approaches to achieving the equality we all strived for: there was Martin Luther King and his followers practicing nonviolence, marching across bridges and getting washed down the street with fire hoses and beaten bloody by big, burly police; and there was Malcolm X, Bobby Seal, Eldridge Cleaver, and the Black Panthers reaching for the same goal, "By any means necessary."

The music of the time reflected the moods and the movement. James Brown's "Say It Loud, I'm Black and I'm Proud," Marvin Gaye's "What's Goin' On," Nina Simone's "Mississippi Goddamn," and the Last Poets' "When the Revolution Comes." They, along with the Panthers and other Black Pride organizations were trying to create solidarity and pride among young Black men and women and at the same time address this intra-racial crime we were cursed with. It came out later that J. Edgar Hoover and the FBI thought the Panthers were being too successful, which led to their infiltration by the FBI and their eventual demise.

At the time, many of the brothers in the military thought MLK was too soft in his approach and questioned what could be achieved by nonviolence. We saw news clips of Black folks marching through towns who, after getting beaten bloody by police and having dogs set upon them, would stand back up and keep marching with heads held high. We saw angry White folks spitting on them and calling them names. I was dismayed by the hate and anger in these White people's eyes and could not help but wonder how they had gotten that much hate within them. We didn't want any part of that game; we didn't see the sense in it.

Most of the brothers I hung out with in the military were from the streets, and being from the streets, had grown up with violence as a way of life, a way of getting things done. Add to that the fact that many of them had been trained to be so-called "killing machines" by the Army. So, letting someone beat on them was not in their character.

There was systemic racism in the military at that time, sometimes subtle and sometimes blatant. Many of the officers looked upon Black soldiers as below them not only in rank, but also in intelligence and status. If you walked into the officers' dining room, you would see most of the waiters were Black men and women dressed in white uniforms and white gloves. Close your eyes, and you'd think you were back in the old Confederacy.

With all this history, we sided with Malcolm X and the faction that preached defending yourself "by whatever means necessary." We organized some of the brothers in and around our Army base along with Samoans, Mexicans, and Puerto Ricans. This is when we started wearing our hair in the Afro hairstyles, and when the Black Power salute signaled solidarity among brothers and sisters.

It came to a head one day when I was in the mess hall, just finishing my meal. For some reason a White guy felt it necessary to tell me, "Nigger, take your tray up to the counter." Without a second thought, I jumped up and knocked him to the ground. He should have stayed down, but he came at me again, and I directed my built-up frustrations over Fort Gordon, Georgia; Norwood, Ohio; Whites-only water fountains; strange fruit; the dehumanizing and humiliation that my father and other Black folks have been subjected to over the last four hundred years—against him. It was an instant reaction coming from my lizard brain and the veracity of my actions surprised everyone, including me.

He ended up in the hospital.

Later that day, as I was walking past the barracks, some of his buddies yelled out, "We're gonna get us a nigger tonight."

Well, I had heard that one before, but this time I wasn't alone. The tension on military posts was thick enough to cut with a chainsaw and when some of the brothers on the post heard what was happening and converged on the barracks, the post exploded with pent-up violence. Words were exchanged, fists flew and pent-up frustration was released resulting in injury and property damage.

When I was called up before the post commander for what had happened, he started in on me about conduct unbecoming of a soldier. I listened for a while—then I let him know he had a problem, and it wasn't just me. I think he wasn't used to enlisted men talking to him like that, especially Black enlisted men, but I had something to say, and I was going to say it. At some point, the Honolulu newspaper got wind of what had happened, picked it up, and ran a story on it with my picture and that of a couple other Black soldiers. The Army realized they indeed had a problem and they had better deal with it—and me. I don't know why I didn't go to the brig for that one. I think they realized they needed to address the issue, or it was going to lead to much bigger problems.

At the time, I had a top-secret security clearance as part of my assignment was to escort warheads—which I assumed were nuclear—to silos in certain areas of the island. They took that away and demoted me in rank, but they then asked for a list of demands the African American troops would like to see. So, I organized a committee of minority soldiers on base to create a list of demands. When we were done, we submitted our list to the commander. We were able to get Black products in the PX, wear our hair the way we wanted, and a few other things, but more importantly, they started listening to us.

After this incident, I had to do some soul-searching. I wasn't proud of what I had done; I hadn't been raised to be like that. I felt I was playing into someone else's hand by reacting to that word and using violence as the way to express myself. It didn't feel good to me, and I vowed to never allow anyone to get me to that point again with that word. I don't want to be at the mercy of someone being able to pull my strings by uttering it. I decided it would have no meaning to me. I don't use it anymore (except in this book), and if I hear it, I might address it verbally if I feel it's worth my time—or I might just ignore it. The "N" word has lost its power.

"Nigger" doesn't describe who I am. It's a word used to perpetuate the myth colonists created to allow them to treat African slaves in a manner akin to how they treated their livestock—only worse. It describes a myth they circulated among themselves to assure themselves that they were better than us and we were beneath them. It's a word that they urged poor whites to use to differentiate us from them and keep us separate. That word or its meaning does not describe me, my family, or anyone I know except he who utters it.

Nigger brings images of beatings and lynchings, nigger means you have no respect for me, nigger means you think you are better than me even if facts prove otherwise;

If I best you in sports, you can resort to nigger

If I am your equal in business you can resort to nigger

If I best you in in academics you can resort to nigger.

Nigger is something that someone told you to say, and by the very act of speaking the word, it offers proof you are at a stage in your evolution where you still need it. Your power lies in my reaction, and you won't get one from me. I never have been and never will be your nigger.

An insult only has power if you acknowledge it.

Later in life I realized how much strength and bravery it takes to engage in nonviolent protest, knowing there's a chance you might get beat up or maybe even die. Now I look at videos of old Black folks and young teenagers both black and white being bloodied by big, burly cops on horseback and think, that's bravery, and that's what happens when you feel like you have nothing to lose.

At some point I had to give credence to the nonviolent protesting and agree that it, along with the things Malcolm X and the Panthers preached, contributed to making some real strides, but I think it took both approaches to wake America up to the fact that we were serious and were not going to just go quietly into the night and let White society continue with the injustices they had practiced for the last four hundred years. The very fact that people are out in the streets protesting, knowing they are going to be subjected to abuse, should give some indication this is not going away until we get equality.

Chapter 15

MARTIN LUTHER KING – 1968

APRIL 4, 1968, I was headed home on leave from the Army when I heard the news: Reverend Martin Luther King had been assassinated. Reverend King had spent his life trying to broker a peaceful resolution to the racial inequalities in this country. The rumor was that Dr. King was being too successful in his attempts at uniting the races and calling worldwide attention to the unequal racial situation in America, and so the White American establishment had to stop him, hence his assassination. Here is an excerpt from Dr. King's "I Have a Dream" speech, which I believe was part of what led to his assassination:

"I have a dream that one day on the red hills of Georgia, sons of former slaves and the sons of former slave-owners will be able to sit down together at the table of brotherhood."

—Dr. Martin Luther King, Jr.

And that would have been the worst nightmare for those in power.

There was a sense of helplessness as the Black communities digested what had just happened. Black leaders took the stage, trying to diffuse the tension.

When I got home, I checked in with my parents, called my girlfriend, and then went and picked up my homeboys. Reverend Shuttlesworth was speaking at one of the community centers over in Avondale, urging people to remain calm and try to find a peaceful resolution. To most Black folks, Dr. King had been the attempt at a peaceful resolution, and now he was dead at the hand of a White dude. In their minds, they had tried the peaceful resolution, and that hadn't worked. We were all frustrated. True, we had made some progress, but it seemed like every time we took a step forward, they—whoever the hell "they" were—did something to thwart our efforts.

We decided to go over to Avondale to see what was happening. We arrived at the corner of Rockdale and Reading Road to see a crowd gathered, listening to various speakers. The tension in the air was as thick as cold Crisco; there were folks circulating throughout the crowd trying to calm people down and keep things from getting out of hand. It was working for a while, but then someone threw a rock and broke the window of a store across the street. People streamed into the store, grabbing things, turning over shelves. It was like someone had popped the plug on a pressure cooker—all hell broke loose. Molotov cocktails appeared out of nowhere; stores were set on fire; cars were overturned; more windows were broken; and people started looting. Nothing to do with Black Power or equality—just frustration.

I grabbed my crew and said, "Get in the car. We're getting out of here."

When one of them started protesting, I said, "Do whatever the hell you want, man, but this bus is leaving; this shit doesn't have anything to do with the Power movement, and I don't want any part of it."

We piled into my convertible, not even bothering to open the doors—just vaulting into the seats. I burned rubber getting out of there. I knew what was coming: police lines, tear gas, the National Guard. We headed back over to Evanston and found there was shit going down there, too. People were using the riot as an excuse to commit crimes against people who couldn't afford the damage. But it was also about the frustration of the failure of using peaceful means to get White America to acknowledge the systemic racism and injustices still suffered by Blacks in this country every day, and about the molasses pace our attempts at overcoming these injustices were moving at.

I got a call from Michelle and Sandy, two friends from College Hill who were stuck in Avondale and needed to get out, so I got in the car, picked them up, and was headed out of Avondale when another car ran a stop sign. I T-boned him. It was an older White guy who had the misfortune of finding himself in the middle of an all-Black neighborhood during a raging race riot. I got out and approached him. We heard shouts and gunfire nearby. He was pan-icked, and I didn't blame him. I calmed him down and assessed the damage to his car. His front bumper was pushed against his tire in a way that made it impossible for him to drive. I knew that if some of the rioters came upon him, it wouldn't be pretty, so I took my tire-iron and pried his bumper away from his tire, gave him my contact information, and told him to get the hell out of there. I didn't have to say it twice. I heard from him the next day. He spent several minutes telling me how scared he had been and thanking me for bailing him out.

When I returned home it was dark. I parked my car and was walking to the front door when a Chevy truck full of Norwood White guys slowed, and I heard "Hey, Nigger" from one of them. I turned to face them and put my hand in my waistband as if reaching for a gun, and they sped off. I'm glad none of them had guns, or I probably wouldn't be sitting here writing this. It was discouraging to see the incredibly deep divide between the races so prevalent in the mainland.

Some of my friends weren't so sensible about things. My friend D and a car full of guys decided to run a National Guard barricade. He came back with six bullet holes in his car door. He was extremely lucky no one in the car was hurt or killed, but D never had the sense he was born with. Later, after I had left Cincy, I heard he was shot and killed—another reason I stopped asking about old friends in the neighborhood and how they were doing.

The riots were not just about the assassination of Dr. King. This was a culmination of four hundred years of trying the peaceful solutions, using diplomacy and nonviolent demonstrations, and trying to talk, talk, talk. It was like trying to get an old, stubborn mule to pay attention to you to no avail and finally having to haul off and whack him upside the head and then say, "NOW LISTEN!" The riots were the last line in the exposition of the race conversation, after the first half of the paragraph had been ignored.

A riot is the expression of exasperation of the unheard after centuries of attempted discourse with the ruling class. A riot is a result of the feeling of helplessness from being mistreated by the judicial system, from being beat up and killed by cops, and from realizing the other side could do whatever they hell the wanted to us without fear of recrimination. While I did not agree with the destruction of businesses and property in our own neighborhood, I did understand the rage that caused it.

It reminds me of the time one of my friends, during an argument with his wife, picked up his prized custom-made guitar and smashed it against the wall, shattering it to pieces.

I later asked him, "Why in the hell would you do that? Why didn't you smash something of hers?"

He said, "She knows how much I love my guitar; I thought by my act of destroying it, she would have to know just how pissed I was."

That doesn't make sense, but I understand the reasoning, and that pretty much describes how people had gotten to the stage of burning their own neighborhoods – it was the equivalent of them smashing their guitars.

After my leave was over, I returned to my post in Hawaii with mixed feelings. Even with the racism that was rampant in the Army, Hawaii was a utopia compared to what was going on the mainland. On the one hand, I was encouraged by the progress that had been made—but I was also frustrated and disillusioned by the efforts of the system to stop this progress. I couldn't hate all White people; that would mean lowering myself to the level of those who profess to be intelligent, free-thinking people while still indulging in the non-sensical act of hating an entire group of people based on a myth that tells them they are better than each and every member of another segment of humanity, without ever knowing them. If that sounds incongruous to you, you are right. It is.

I knew all White people were not involved in this suppression, but I knew there were some who would do anything they could to impede Black progress. These were the folks we needed to deal with. But I knew it was not something that was going to happen overnight. It was going to have to be a social, cultural, and psycho-logical evolution that was going to take more time than I have here on earth.

So, for the time being, I decided to party instead.

Chapter 16

HONOLULU, HAWAII

H ONOLULU, TO ME, WAS like another world. Everyone was smiling and talking openly with each other, even complete strangers. Approaching a stranger on the street with a question would elicit an honest answer; ask for directions, and they would sometimes even walk with you to make sure you got there.

Standing in line at a local grocery store, I looked around and realized that within my sight there was an incredible mix of colors, ethnicities, and nationalities, and for the first time, as a person of color, I wasn't a minority! So many different cultures; food from virtually every country; so many religions, spiritualities, and philosophies! Languages I had never heard before and an array of people of every shade of color—most of them darker than white. I was loving it!

This was the '60s and, like much of the country, Honolulu was buzzing. My mind was a giant balloon; my consciousness was expanding at an incredible rate just from talking to folks on the street—which I did at every opportunity. I was soaking up the exposure to different cultures and to people from every walk of life all getting along, working together, socializing, and exchanging ideas, foods, and culture.

But the thing I loved most about Honolulu was the variety of beautiful women—I was in awe! They came to Honolulu from all over the world; there were French women with their beautiful accents, African women with lovely deep brown eyes and the poise of queens, Brazilian women with their gorgeous copper-colored skin, and tall, athletic Dutchwomen. There were Jamaican women with their sexy lilt, Polynesian women with long, flowing hair, and vibrant German women; they all came through Honolulu.

And then there was Camille: a tall, Creole beauty with reddish-blond curly hair down to her waist and a body to die for. When she passed, she took the breath out of every red-blooded man in sight. The heavens opened and provided a soft cushion of clouds for her to walk on; her hips swayed like a pendulum, and if you allowed your gaze to linger too long, you could be hypnotized and walk into a pole. Her booty had a complex jiggle that was impossible to describe, but suffice it to say, it stopped men in their tracks. She smelled like the essence of every fragrant flower. Her lovely green eyes were set in almond-shaped sockets, and her face would have made Cleopatra want to go back to beauty school.

Men would involuntarily stop and stare slack-jawed, even when their wives were with them. I saw a guy stumble and begin mumbling incoherent shit, drool forming on his lips. The sight of Camille had sucked his brains out.

Get what I'm saying? Camille was fine!

But there was one small problem: the girl was crazy. I don't mean mental hospital crazy. She was street crazy—and that's even worse. Mental hospital crazy is something that "happens" to people. Something goes sideways in their brains, and most times they don't even realize it has happened.

Street crazy is premediated. It's not something that has happened to someone unknowingly or unwillingly; it's something they themselves have decided to be and then acted upon it. Street-crazy people seem innocent enough and blend in with the rest of us until something sets them off—then someone gets hurt or somebody dies.

Meeting Camille for the first time you wouldn't have had a clue she was crazy—until something bent her the wrong way, and it came out.

She was thirty-two and hot as a hare in heat; I was eighteen and having a hard time keeping up with her. I was like a junky, and she was the needle. I was in over my head. I knew I should be walking away, but it was just too good. I was strung out, so I kept coming back for more.

She introduced me to fine wines and all manner of things that made an impressionable young man like me feel good. She took me to fine restaurants, fed me the foods of the gods: things like escargot, scampi, and French cuisine so exquisite I wanted to cry. She exposed me to things I never would have dreamed were in existence, and then she'd whisper soft French words in my ear that I didn't understand but that still turned my insides to Jell-O.

But like I said, the girl was crazy.

Here's an example of when the crazy came out in Camille. One night we were at a party at a friend's house, joking around, when one of the dudes at the party must have grabbed her ass or something. Swish—click—before anybody knew it, she had a six-inch butterfly knife at his throat, saying, "I'll cut your goddamn throat, mother-fucker."

She had gone from the fun-loving Camille to a cold-blooded, steely-eyed Creole bitch that I didn't even know. The guy's eyes got as big as saucers, and he looked at me for help. I shrugged my shoulders and said, "Man, you better back off and apologize or something, 'cause this shit is out of my hands."

Our relationship came to a head one night when we were in her condo lying in bed; there was a loud banging at the door. I turned to her and said, "Who the hell is that?"

She looked out the window and said, "Oh, that's my husband."

I looked at her in astonishment and said, "I didn't know you were married!"

She said, "Oh, we're separated. He just hasn't gotten over it."

"So, what are we gonna do?" I whispered.

"You probably shouldn't go to the door because he usually has his gun," she said matter-of-factly. "I'll just go and tell him to leave me alone."

I said, "Wait, wait a minute, baby. Why don't we just stay here and pretend like nobody's home?" She was pissed off; I knew what she was like when she was pissed—and I didn't want her to get us both killed. I finally convinced her to stay in the bedroom without saying a word.

He hung out at the front door for a while; he was drunk, and I knew he was still strung out on Camille and I understood why. After a while he finally went away.

I had to make a decision; meeting Camille was one of the most gratifying things that had ever happened to my young, impressionable eighteen-year-old self, she was way out of my league. But something inside told me if I stayed with her, she was going to get me killed or in serious trouble.

I tried telling her it was over with us. She did not take it well. She told me that if she couldn't have me, nobody would. I didn't know what to read into that statement; I guess I didn't want to believe what I thought she meant. So, from then on, I treated Camille like poison and stayed as far away from her as I could. If she was on one side of the island, I made sure I was on the other; if she came in the front door at a party, I went out the back.

I was young, full of juice, and ready to cut loose, but without the wisdom to go with it. That was my first introduction to the great big world outside of my little Midwest life and I realized that I had a <u>lot</u> to learn.

Chapter 17

HAWAII LIFESTYLE

Surfer Dude

I WAS AMAZED AT the clarity of the ocean in Hawaii. I had never experienced a body of water where you could see more than a foot in front of your face while underwater. The ocean and the reefs around Hawaii fascinated me with the thousands of colorful fish, dolphins, and huge whales. It was the stuff I had seen on television, but that had never quite seemed real, just something on the screen in the living room. I guess it never occurred to me it really existed or that I would experience it.

For the first four years in Hawaii, I was in the water six days a week and, after that, every chance I could get. I loved snorkeling, scuba diving, spear fishing, board surfing, boogie boarding, and body surfing.

I met and started hanging out with some local guys: Big John, Boom, Kimo and some other locals from Waimanalo. Having grown up on the islands, they were comfortable with every aspect of the ocean as it was a big part of their culture. They taught me how to harvest the delicious opihi, Hawaii's deadliest seafood, so called because so many people have died trying to harvest them. They grow on the sides of rocks in the ocean, and to harvest them you usually find yourself either being in the water with the waves threatening to wash you out to sea, or clinging precariously to the rocks with one hand while trying to pry the delicacy from the rocks while the same waves are trying to bash you against the rocks. But they are worth the risk! I carried a saltshaker with me in case I happened upon a good opihi harvesting area. Once you have experienced this Hawaiian treat, you're hooked.

We'd swim out to the reef and drop down into the deep water on the other side to search along the back side of the reef for grouper, *kumu* (Hawaii goatfish), *uku* (Hawaii blue-green snapper), and untold numbers of other fish that populate Hawaii's reefs.

We were out night diving with underwater lights when I realized there were several sharks circling around our group of divers. I tapped one of my friends on the back and motioned excitedly to the sharks. We surfaced, and he said, "Eh—no worries, bruh. Only da kine sand shark—de no boda you."

I wasn't totally convinced, but it didn't seem to bother them, so I continued diving—all the while looking over my shoulder. The sharks were more interested in our catch, which we always kept on a line some distance from our bodies, than in us.

A short while after I arrived in Hawaii, I bought my first surfboard, a massive twelve-foot Cadillac of a board on which I surfed the waves of Waikiki. Waikiki has a long, gentle, rolling break that starts far offshore and rolls almost all the way in to shore. This was before someone had a brain-fart and thought of attaching a leash from your ankle to the board so that when you fell off, the board stayed with you. We didn't have leashes, so when you lost your board on one of the outside breaks, you had a long swim to retrieve it unless someone caught it and held it for you.

I graduated to smaller and smaller boards until I found myself on the north shore of Hawaii at the famous Bonsai Pipeline. It was a beautiful swell, with good offshore winds holding the face up; a sunny day, fantastic surf, a joint—who could ask for anything better?

If you get high enough, you can convince yourself you are capable of just about anything. Sitting on the beach at the Pipeline, stoned out of my mind, watching the big waves breaking in the shallow water, I convinced myself I could handle the Pipeline break. I paddled out beyond the break, waited for the perfect wave, paddled, paddled, and caught it! I was at the top of the wave, sliding down the steep slope, what a rush, nothing like it in the world—then I pearled and wiped out. Tons of water came crashing down on me and took me to the bottom. I didn't know which way was up. I got scraped along the shallow coral bottom for a bit, and just when I was about to run out of air, I was spat back out into the foamy whitewater.

I swam to shore, retrieved my board, and sat there for a while contemplating what had just happened. Most sane people would have gotten up, drove away, and called it a day, but I wasn't going to let a wave kick my ass, so I decided to get back in the saddle. I grabbed my board and out I went again to slay the savage beast.

I caught a beautiful, curling wave. I got up and positioned myself, but this time I got sucked up and over the falls. I had experienced going over the falls before, but not on a wave this big. It was like getting pummeled by a gang of angry Sumo wrestlers, being thrown off a cliff, bouncing off the rocks below, then coming up and getting hit full on in the face with a fire hose. I made it through the foam to shore and found my board broken in two. It was like Mother Maui was trying to tell me I wasn't ready, so I decided to listen. I threw my board in the nearest dumpster, packed up my shit, and left.

And that my friend, was the end of my surfing days.

Chapter 18

MUSIC

B ACK IN MY HOOD in Cincy, I had sung in a couple of different groups, but we were mostly limited to singing on the street corners or occasionally in civic centers. Those gigs sometimes ended up in a gang fight, or someone would fire off a couple of rounds and everyone would head for the back door or the bathroom. It's amazing how many people you can pack into the bathroom when someone is firing off shots outside.

At Fort Shafter, I met Tommy Sullivan—a good-looking, smooth-talking crooner from Memphis, Tennessee. Tommy could talk the sweet out of sugar and dance like Bojangles. Tommy was a good singer and so was I, so we naturally gravitated to each other. We started harmonizing in our free time; then another good friend, Frank Guerrero (Cowboy), joined up with us, and we had some nice three-part harmonies going. We added a bass player, a horn, a guitar, and drums. We called ourselves the Diplomats of Soul, which we later shortened to the Diplomats.

The drinking age in Hawaii was eighteen at the time, so I was as good as being an adult. We began performing in a few of the bars and clubs downtown and on some of the military bases. The downtown gigs were cool, but with the war going on, everyone on the military bases was on edge, and it didn't take much to initiate a fight. When the fights started, we'd just close the curtains, sit back, and hang out.

One day, Cowboy got the thing we all dreaded: orders for Vietnam. Cowboy was a little crazy and pretty much fearless. We figured he would head to Nam, come back a year later, and we'd continue. That one year of overseas duty passed quickly, and on the day he was scheduled to arrive in Honolulu, I went to pick up his wife and baby boy to go to the airport to meet him. We were getting ready to head out the door when she got the word: Cowboy was not coming home, except in a body bag. He had taken a Jeep out joyriding with a couple of other soldiers to celebrate his last day in-country, hit a mine, and died from his injuries.

The mood went from joyful anticipation to mourning. As much as I was dismayed at the news, I had to keep it together enough to help his wife get through this. What do you say to someone who has just lost the love of her life and the father of her child? There are only so many ways to say "I'm sorry" or "This really sucks."

Years later I visited "The Wall" and went to get a rubbing of his name. I broke down crying and couldn't stop. I thought I had gotten over it, but I guess I had never taken time to process his death. It brought back all the frustrations of seeing young men in their prime dying or coming home mentally and physically crippled for life because of some politician's senseless war. When my son was eighteen years old, I looked at him and his friends and realized this was the age of the fresh-faced young kids the United States had been sending to Vietnam as cannon fodder. I shuddered at the thought.

Our band, the Diplomats, continued. We were a smooth R&B group with two high-stepping, smooth-talking crooners up front and a jamming five-piece band backing us up. We started attracting attention around town and began opening for some of the big names that came through town: the Four Tops, Buddy Miles, Lou Rawls, Ink Spots, Rufus Thomas. We started hanging out with people like Curtis Mayfield, the Impressions, and the Jazz Crusaders. We were living the life, getting a taste of how the rich and famous lived—only we were neither rich nor famous. But it was a good time in my life.

When Tommy got his discharge, he moved back to Memphis, and I started singing in some of the posh clubs and hotels in downtown Honolulu. One of these was a famous five-star restaurant that had a clientele that included some of the wealthiest people in the world. Everything was first-class, from the décor to the level of service. The number of drop-dead gorgeous women in attendance was breathtaking.

The piano bar had seats for ten to twelve people, and there were dark, cozy booths set back far enough so an outsider couldn't distinguish who was there or what they were doing. After playing there for a bit, I realized the room had a surprisingly good turnover, and there was a pattern to this turnover. Some of these beauties were not there just for fun.

Being on stage, I had a ringside seat to watch happenings in the club. It took a while for me to realize what was going on. One night, a single guy walked in and had a seat at the piano bar. Soon one of the beauties approached him. Her breasts brushed lightly against him as she slid into the seat next to him, making sure he got a whiff of her expensive perfume. She leaned over, whispered into his ear, and after a brief pause, rose and left the club. He paused for a moment, and with an elated look on his face—kinda like he had just hit the jackpot for fifty million—rose, paid his tab, and followed. After a surprisingly brief period, she returned looking for other needs to satisfy.

I noticed well-dressed businessmen visiting from the mainland being accompanied by stunningly beautiful women half their age. Then the next week another patron would stroll in with the same lady on his arm.

After a bit, I got to know some of these ladies. I enjoyed hanging out with them, and we gravitated to each other, maybe from us all being in the entertainment business. They were collectively one of the most well-spoken, well-mannered, cultured group of people I have ever met. They explained to me that because of the clientele they served, they needed to be able to converse intelligently on virtually any subject that came up whether it was sports, financial markets, politics, current events or whatever.

We hung out together after-hours, swapping stories and laughing. Some of their stories were hilarious! Someone should write a book on the foibles and bloopers of that profession. It would surely be a bestseller! The amount of money they ended up with at the end of the night was staggering, too! Some of them were working their way through college; some were supporting a family; some were just having fun with it. Some were in it for the long haul—or as long as their good looks held up. Some had a monetary goal in mind and when they reached it, they just disappeared.

***

Honolulu in the '60s was like the Wild, Wild West, where pretty much anything was okay. There were very few limits. I know they call Las Vegas "Sin City," but Vegas had nothing on Honolulu. This was a time of free love and partying until the lights went out, which they never did. There was little or no censorship in the clubs, at the movies, or on the streets. Drugs flowed freely. I saw a lot of things I had never seen before and did a lot of things I'll never do again. Whatever your pleasure, whatever your game was—there was something, someone, somewhere in Honolulu to satisfy your needs.

The air was electric. There were protests against the Vietnam war, protests for civil rights, and protests for the sake of protesting. There was a wave of awakening sweeping across America, and when it reached Honolulu, it was full-blown.

I'm your momma, I'm your
daddy
I'm that nigga in the alley
I'm your doctor when you
need

Want some coke, have some
weed
You know me, I'm your friend
Your main boy, thick and
thin
I'm your pusherman
I'm your pusherman
—from Curtis Mayfield's
"Pusher Man," *Superfly*
album

I had a tricked-out van I named "Happiness" because it was my party bus. I'd hit Kalakaua Avenue around midnight, attired in striped bell-bottoms, a leather vest with no shirt, a wide-brimmed leather hat, with rose-tinted granny glasses hanging on the tip of my nose and stylish leather shoes with 3-inch heels. I'd cruise the strip from Kapiolani Park to the Ala Wai, blasting Sly and the Family Stone's "Higher" or Santana's "Samba Pa Ti" from the stereo and leaving a trail of smoke billowing out of the windows. You could get a contact high just standing near Happiness.

"Hey, man, what's it gonna be? Weed? Got some good bud, speed, acid—just got some killer sunshine!" Sometimes I would end up with a busload of people stoned out of their minds.

One night, I had backed over something in the driveway and lost my back bumper. My girlfriend Kari and I were on our way down to the strip when we got flashed by HPD. We knew why he pulled us over, so we quickly jumped out, went back to the cruiser, and explained, all in one breath, "We just lost our bumper, and we realize we shouldn't be driving around without a bumper, so we're on our way back home to park it until we can get it fixed."

The fact is, if he had gotten close to Happiness, he would have had good reason for searching her, and I was holding a BUNCH of drugs that night.

Fortunately for us, the police officer was in a good mood. He told us he wasn't going to ticket us if we went straight home. We assured him that home is indeed where we were headed. He drove off. We continued down to the strip to begin our night of partying, thinking there was no way that cop was going to end up near us again because we were in Kalihi when he stopped us. The strip was miles away.

We continued our night of partying, hitting the clubs, cruising the strip, and then—damn—fucking blue lights again! We jumped out, ran back to the cop, and started explaining, "Officer, we just lost our bumper, and we are headed..." Then we realized it was the same cop!

I straightened up, dumbfounded, at a loss for words; by then we both really had a buzz going. I was okay for a minute. I held it together, taking deep breaths to keep from laughing. We stood there doing our best to not appear stoned. But keeping down the laugh building up inside me was like taking a big hit on a pipe and trying to hold it in when you know you have to cough. I was okay until Kari snorted, which she sometimes did when she was about to laugh. That did it. We both burst out laughing.

The cop sat there and looked at us for a minute like we were crazy. Luckily, he had a sense of humor or just didn't want to deal with it.

When we finally stopped laughing, he said, "Just get your ass off the street, and don't let me catch you again."

This time we did go straight home.

Chapter 19

BACK TO CINCINNATI

YOU CAN ONLY PARTY for so long and after a while partying ran its course with me. In 1971, I moved back to Cincinnati with my new wife and daughter and bought a distributorship with the 7 Up bottling company. When I first started with 7 Up, part of my route took me into the hills and hollers of Kentucky. It was a part of Kentucky where it was obvious that they were not used to seeing Black folks in the flesh. There was one pony keg I delivered to; an old, dilapidated shack built on stilts, with a rusted metal roof that sounded thunderous when it rained; old, weathered wood siding turned gray with age; and a porch made from rough-sawn timber with no rails so folks could back their trucks up to the deck to load their cases of beer and whisky. It was off the main road and up a rutted gravel driveway lined with maple and oak trees, with a wide dirt parking area at the end.

The first time I drove up, an old man was sitting on the front porch, smoking a pipe and rocking in his chair as if he had not a care in the world. He wore worn coveralls and old, leather boots laced halfway up. His skin was tan and wrinkled, and his hat sat on top of a mop of short, stringy hair. An old hound dog with floppy ears and droopy eyes was at his side.

He recognized the truck when I drove up, but when I got out and he saw who—or what—I was, he instinctively reached for his shotgun just inside the door. I reassured him I was just there to deliver his soda, not to rob him. I'm sure I was the first Black person he had ever seen in those parts, and he didn't know what to make of me. He looked slightly embarrassed but still on edge.

I walked inside the store to take inventory, and he proceeded to tell me how the niggers and Jews were fucking up the country and how glad he was there were none around here. I listened while I stocked his shelf and took his empties out to the truck. I collected what he owed, walked out the door, noticing the old vintage double-barrel shotgun sitting next to his chair, and drove off to my next stop.

My route took me to his pony keg once a week, and each week he had another story about the niggers, Jews, Commies, or some other threat to the country. I didn't respond to his words as I knew he was just trying to get a reaction out of me. Instead, I began asking questions about him, his family, how he grew up—you know, just conversational stuff. Little by little we got to know each other, and bit by bit he began letting his guard down.

He had fought in World War II, and I got the feeling he had seen some things he wished he hadn't. The Army had been his only experience with the outside world, and after that he had come back to hole up in his holler. Other than the time he spent in the Army he had spent his entire life there in Kentucky in his little holler. His view of the outside world was limited to conversations with patrons of his store and the area's weekly newspaper, which was slanted in one direction—to the right.

As the weeks went by, our conversations began getting deeper and more involved. I knew I had his curiosity piqued when he began pulling up a stool for me when I drove up, almost like he was looking forward to our talks.

Through our conversations on his front porch he got to know my world, and I got to know his. Through our talks we realized that in some ways, we had a lot of things in common, and in some ways, not so much. There were things we agreed upon and some we didn't. We were able to acknowledge that we were from two different worlds, but more importantly, that neither was a threat to the other. I didn't fit the image of a Black man he had carried with him for his entire life, which made him even more curious.

We went on like this for a few months until I got my permanent distributorship and another route. I didn't see him again until I stopped into his pony keg to say goodbye a couple of weeks before I was to leave Cincinnati and move back to Hawaii. He invited me in and commenced to telling me how he considered me a friend and would like to come and see me off at the airport when I left. Of course, I didn't really expect him to, since he never left his holler—but I was touched by the fact that he wanted to.

It's more important now than ever for Americans to have conversations with each other. It is imperative that we bridge the gap that separates us so we can understand other cultures. We need to get beyond the sensationalism so prevalent in the media today. Things get twisted around according to which media you read or listen to. When an event occurs in the U.S. today, you get a completely different take from Fox News and Newsmax than you would from PBS, MSNBC or the *New York Times*. Some media leans left, and some leans right—we need to look at the gray area, in the middle. The truth usually lies in there somewhere.

We can get to those truths by having one-on-one conversations, listening more than talking, and stepping outside of the need to be right. That even includes accepting that in some situations, there is no right or wrong. We don't have to agree with each other; we just need to consider the other's point of view. Everyone comes with their own experiences, giving them a distinct slant on things. In trying to grasp what the other sees, you can't help but open your mind a bit. Otherwise, we are like a tree that keeps cutting off its limbs to spite itself; this can only lead to the whole tree dying.

On a macro view it is ridiculous for all Republicans to take a stand against Democrats just because they are Democrats and vice versa. At some point you have to look at whether this is healthy for the country and whether we can come to a consensus for the good of the country rather than stopping progress because of any particular ideology. That is just as asinine as a White person hating all Black people just because they are Black. I still cannot fathom how you can hate an individual you have never met—someone who has never done anything offending to you—just because of their race.

I can accept there are some folks whose views are far enough from mine that we may never really see eye to eye. But for me to hate that person and wish them harm because of their views, race or their religion? I hope I never get to that point; I don't want that kind of poison in my heart.

I had lasted in Cincinnati for around a year but Hawaii kept calling and finally, back to Hawaii I went.

Chapter 20

SPIRITS

"*'IT IS REQUIRED OF every man,' the ghost returned, 'that the spirit within him should walk abroad among his fellow men, and travel far and wide; and if that spirit goes not forth in life, it is condemned to do so after death.'*"

—Charles Dickens

"*During the day, I don't believe in ghosts. At night, I'm a little more open-minded.*"

—Unknown

The existence of spirits and demons are noted in every culture; every civilization in recorded history has acknowledged them in some form or other. Folks who have lived in Hawaii for any time and who have explored the islands beyond the regular tourist areas can attest to the existence of local spirits. Hawaiians are careful not to anger these spirits. I had experienced spirits before, and I knew they existed. It wasn't something I dwelled on or worried about—just something I was aware of.

For three years, I lived in a wonderful old plantation house in Waikapu, Maui. The Maui plantation houses were built to house the sugarcane workers and were typically one-story, wood-framed houses sitting on wood stilts. This particular house was over a hundred years old and sat at the end of a rutted dirt driveway surrounded by a medley of mango, breadfruit, and banana trees. On one side was Mr. Rogers, who raised cows and pigs, and next door lived the Naole family, a beautiful Hawaiian family who had the most fantastic luaus and who would share anything and everything they had with me. It was surrounded by sugarcane fields, which was nice except when the sugar cane company burned the fields without warning, whereupon we would grab what we could for the day and make a break for it along the narrow driveway, flames on both sides, choking from the thick black smoke.

The house didn't have a locking door. It had screens but no windows, and there was a hole in the floor where we threw our whisky bottles and beer cans. About once every six months, once they'd reached from the ground up to the floor level, we'd flip a coin to see who was going to crawl under the house to clear out all the bottles and cans.

One of my favorite features of the house was an outdoor toilet located in a small closet-like structure with three walls, a roof and no door. The open doorway faced Haleakala mountain, so when I sat down for my morning constitutional, my view included the majestic Haleakala directly in front of me, Maalaea Harbor on the right, and Kahului Harbor on the left. I think back on those days and realize those were some of the most pleasurable morning movements I've ever experienced; how I miss that commode!

I am sure over the years many different people and families had inhabited that old house; it was well-lived-in. At night I could hear the leaves rustling in the trees and the occasional hooting of an owl. If the wind died down enough, I could hear the termites eating away at the walls. Scorpions, geckos, and centipedes were there long before I came and would be there long after I had left—you just learned to live with them.

Another feature that came with the house was an old spirit. At night when things had quieted down, I could hear him breathing. It was a breath that was difficult to locate; at times I felt as if it emanated from the attic, and then I'd hear it in the next room. Other times it felt as if it were right next to me. After living there for a while, I realized it had an omnipresence that encompassed the whole house, as if it were part of the studs, the walls, the very essence of the house itself.

Sometimes at night I would hear footsteps outside my window. I'd grab my machete and flashlight to investigate, but there was nothing there. One night I even took a blanket and sat outside where I thought the steps were emanating from—only to realize the steps had the same ghostly omnipresence as the breaths inside. It wasn't a malevolent spirit. There was nothing evil about it—it just co-existed in the same space I did. Eventually it became a comforting companion, if that makes sense, and we settled into a peaceful co-existence, occupying the same space for years.

Years later I met a lady who had lived in that same house years before. During our conversation, when she learned where I lived, she paused for a minute. Then she asked, "Hey, is that spirit still there?"

I replied, "You mean the one you can hear breathing in the walls?"

"Yes, that's the one. Don't worry, though; he means no harm to you." She spoke as if talking about an old friend.

I said, "Yes, I can feel that, but thanks for letting me know."

***

My best friend Ward Taylor contracted bone cancer, and after a long and painful fight finally succumbed to that terrible disease. I was in denial for a long time before his death, believing he would suddenly do a turn-around and pop out of bed, totally recovered and saying something like, "I'm just messing with you, man. I was just taking a break."

Wayne Dyer gave the analogy of life as a trolley car where some people get on and then get off at the next stop; some folks might get on, get off for a while and get back on. If you are lucky you will have a few people in your life that get on the trolley and stay on for the whole ride – Ward was supposed to be one of those.

In my mind Ward couldn't die. We had plans to go to Tahiti when we both retired and sit on the beach drinking beer and watching bare-breasted beauties! That had always been the plan.

Finally, after months of denial, I got a call from his daughter. When I picked up the phone, she said, "Ron, you should come. We think he's waiting for you."

I retreated to my room, closed the door, and cried for my friend. I thought about the many nights we had spent watching old movies and drinking coffee laced with Wild Turkey, with the proportion of Wild Turkey to coffee increasing until, at the end of the night, there was nothing but Wild Turkey in our mugs. I'd never again hear his famous one-liners that would send us both into fits of paralyzing laughter, and we'd never be able to fulfill our promise to each other to make that Tahiti excursion.

By the time I got there he was in a coma and couldn't speak but he acknowledged my presence with a movement of his hand toward me when I sat next to his hospital bed. The hospice nurse explained he had one foot on this shore and was being hailed by spirits in the next world. We all said our goodbyes and expressed our deep love. I could feel him relax when we were done.

He died soon after, and at the moment of his passing I felt his presence in the room, hanging around for a while to let us know he was okay. Over the years, I have tried to find words to describe the feeling in that room. Suffice it to say, it was the most peaceful and serene feeling I have ever felt in my life. It was like he was projecting the feeling of the spirit world that he had stepped into. It was such a tranquil feeling that I felt that, if that is what the next phase is like, then sign me up. If I'd ever had a fear of death, it was gone after experiencing that. Now when I look at obituaries, I feel like these folks haven't died—they have been released.

Don't get me wrong, I plan to live out a full and fruitful life—but now I do in some respects look forward to being released after I've accomplished all I'm here to do.

My wife and I sometimes joke that if we wanted to hear from Ward, he'd come in the form of an animal. Once, while walking on the beach, I asked for a sign from Ward, and as if on cue, a seagull dropped to eye level six feet in front of me, riding the wind. I stopped, and he hovered there for a full minute, just looking in my eyes. It wasn't even surprising. I know it was Ward saying, "I love you, man."

Years later, one of my employees warned me that spirits of dead people were constantly making themselves visible to her. Once, after one of our weekly meetings, we dropped into casual conversation, and I started talking about Ward. She stopped and said, "Oh, tall Black guy?" and proceeded to describe Ward to me exactly; there was no way she could have known what he had looked like.

With a shocked look on my face, I said, "How did you know that?"

"He's been hanging around upstairs. I was wondering what he wanted," she said matter-of-factly.

Chapter 21

DEMONS

"*WHAT IF SOME DAY or night a demon were to steal after you into your loneliest loneliness and say to you: 'This life as you now live it and have lived it, you will have to live once more and innumerable times more'... Would you not throw yourself down and gnash your teeth and curse the demon who spoke thus? Or have you once experienced a tremendous moment when you would have answered him: 'You are a god, and never have I heard anything more divine.'"*

——**Friedrich Nietzsche**

I have felt spirits and been around people who could feel spirits in various degrees most of my life, so I acknowledge their existence and feel fine with coexisting with them.

Demons, on the other hand, were a concept I had never experienced directly. There are stories of demons prowling for souls to inhabit and preying upon people at difficult and weak moments in their lives. In ancient Near Eastern religions, as well as Abrahamic and Christian religions, demons were considered harmful spiritual entities that could possess people, sometimes calling for exorcisms. In ancient Mesopotamia, there were seven evil deities known as Shedu and represented by winged bulls. Sumerians acknowledged the existence of Galla demons. Ancient Jewish texts talk about the demon Lilith, who was Adam's first wife before Eve. The Catholic Church has an entire division of the church devoted to demons, possessions, and exorcising demons from humans that have been "taken" and possessed by these demons. *The Rite of Exorcism* was first published in 1614 by Pope Paul V. And every Christian knows about their very own devil. I never worried about demons because I always felt I was grounded enough to withstand any onslaught from a malevolent spirit.

It was in the early 70's, and I had just gone through an emotional breakup with my first wife. Divorce is hard to begin with, but it also involved my four-year-old daughter, whom I loved dearly. I was living in my van, trying to figure out what this all meant and how I was going to get on with my life. I was in a very dark and vulnerable state financially, emotionally, and spiritually. My spirit was like an open wound, susceptible to any infectious intrusion that happened upon me.

I usually parked in isolated spots in different areas of Oahu where I wouldn't be disturbed or hassled by the police. One night, I was parked in an area off the beaten path, an old gully where at one time a stream must have meandered through before the water was interrupted and diverted for use in the sugarcane plantations. Surrounded by Koa and Kiawe trees, I was out of sight from anyone passing by. It was a dark, moonless night and I was lying in bed reading by candlelight when I felt a strong presence outside my van.

I opened the door, stepped outside in the night, and saw what I can only describe as an area absent of light, darker than the already dark night. It was a loose-limbed humanoid shape floating above the ground. It hung there for a minute and then began to move toward me. It was preceded by an overpowering sense of evil. Not your everyday bad feeling, but a debilitating, smothering evil, like an ocean of fetid slime. Every cell in my body and every instinct was aroused, and little by little I began to feel as if my body was being enveloped in a large blanket that slowly tightened, stifling movement and cutting off my breath. At the same time, I felt as if someone or something was slowly creeping into my brain, into my soul—probing for a weakness or point of entry.

I sensed that if I let my guard down for the slightest second, I would not be able to maintain my soul as my own, and there would be no returning to life as I knew it. I stood trembling, fighting, and resisting for what seemed like an eternity. I had only one conscious thought: if I didn't stand my ground and maintain my strength, if there was the slightest opening, this entity would enter and invade my very soul.

It was the most evil, malevolent, powerful, all-consuming force I had ever felt—or have felt since. There are no words to describe the overwhelming evil that emanated from this entity, and unless you have been unlucky enough to have been assaulted by the same sense of raw, unrelenting evil—and I hope you never will be—you'll never be able to comprehend it.

I stood there for an indeterminate amount of time—it could have been five minutes, or it could have been five hours; I had no way of knowing. It was a standoff, with it trying to find a weakness, and me trying to muster up every ounce of strength and goodness I could to stave it off.

Eventually, the force began to loosen its hold on me and oozed away into whatever dark hole from whence it came. Drenched in sweat and trembling uncontrollably, I stumbled into my van, completely exhausted. It was as if I had been in a protracted physical, emotional, and psychological battle during which I had had to use every bit of every cell in my body to fight this entity. I closed the door and collapsed on the floor.

I have no idea why this entity chose me. I can only guess that it sensed a weakness in me that it felt it could use as a portal. I had read about similar experiences, but before this they were always just abstract events that happened to someone else. I never for one minute would have imagined something like this happening to me. Since then I have been careful not to do anything that could be construed as an invitation. I don't even watch horror movies dealing with possessions, devils, or other evil beings. Once you have experienced it, it's not an abstract thought anymore. It's real, malevolent, and it scares me beyond anything I've ever encountered.

Chapter 22

HONOLULU 1973

RIGHT AROUND 1973, A producer approached me about moving my music career forward in the recording industry. After some negotiations, I signed a recording contract with ABC Dunhill. They had it in their minds that they were going to make me into a Black Tom Jones or something of that nature. There were several composers writing for me, including Jimmy Web and Douglas Gibbs, and I traveled to L.A. to meet with some of the bigwigs in the recording industry. The promise of stardom was impending, and I was whisked into this world of money, power, and sleaze. I enjoyed it for a while, but it wasn't long before I realized I was pretty much a piece of property to these people. I suspected that my manager had mob connections, but I couldn't quite put my finger on it—just had a feeling. Whatever it was, the more involved I got, the more uneasy I felt about it. Finally I decided that world just wasn't for me so I did a disappearing act and backed out of the deal.

I had been working with Kit Ebersbach, a bespectacled, soft-spoken guy who could be mistaken for a university professor or research scientist if you saw him on the street—I think he may have even worn a pocket protector. But when you put him in front of a keyboard, he'd get a fanatical look in his eyes and proceed to "tear up" the keys. He was a fantastic keyboard player based in Honolulu, and I felt privileged to work with him.

We worked as a duo sometimes, and we also had a tight six-piece jazz band that played in some of the jazz clubs around town. On Sundays we ran a jazz jam session at the Chart House on the bottom floor of the Ilikai hotel on Ala Moana Boulevard, right across from the docks. It was an open-air venue, and we set up right next to the open veranda looking out on the docks full of million-dollar yachts. The Chart House was packed every session; there was always an air of anticipation because you never knew who was going to appear on stage. Musicians from all over the world came to sit in. The energy produced at those jam sessions is still floating in many people's consciousnesses. More than forty years later I still run into people in different parts of the world who talk about those jam sessions.

We were working seven nights a week, sometimes two gigs a day. Right about this time, one of the restaurants/nightclubs we worked in asked us to open a new place on the island of Maui. We jumped at the chance—it was a good excuse to go to the "Valley Isle," which Maui was known as. The restaurant was Nick's Fish Market owned by Nick Nickolas, or "Nick the Greek" as he was known. I don't even know if he was Greek, but that's what we called him. He was a celebrity restaurateur who had locations in Chicago, Honolulu, and Los Angeles.

Nick was a big man who carried himself in a manner that commanded authority—but not intimidation. He always had a smile on his face, and I never heard him yell at anyone, but if he needed to get something across, he had a way of making himself understood. I liked working for him. Nick ran a tight ship, which was important in the restaurant industry because of the slim margins. If you weren't paying attention, a slight rise in minimum wage or food prices could take you by surprise. You could have been out of business six months ago and not even known it. Keeping his eye on the numbers and hiring top-quality waiters, waitresses, and chefs were the reasons he continued to be successful.

So—off to Maui we went.

Chapter 23

MAUI

I HIT MAUI AT the age of twenty-seven, and the John Denver song "Rocky Mountain High" that goes *"He was born in the summer of his twenty-seventh year, coming home to a place he'd never been before"* pretty much describes how I felt when I arrived.

Our airport limo got to the club right around sunset. It was one of those balmy Maui days, eighty degrees with a gentle trade wind blowing from the south, just enough to keep it from being uncomfortable. The scent of plumeria was heavy in the air, and there was the soothing sound of waves lapping against the shore. Nick's was located on the second floor, right across the street from the Lahaina seawall, and we were looking forward to getting into the club to set up our equipment and check acoustics in the room.

We were about to disembark from the limo when we noticed groups of people walking slowly across the street in front of us. They all had slack faces and glazed looks in their eyes as if they were in a trance. Then we saw that shop owners were shutting their doors and proceeding toward the ocean in the same mindless trance. The limo driver got out and succumbed to the same stupor. Everything and everyone seemed to stop.

Had we wandered into the night of the living dead? Had some strange virus infected their minds and turned them into mindless, blank-eyed zombies?

Larry, our drummer, turned in his seat and said, "What the hell is going on here?"

Just when we were about to consider getting the hell out of there, someone said, "Wow! Check out that sunset, man!"

The sky was ablaze in colors: orange, purple, blue, and colors there were no descriptions for. It was like an ongoing light show involving the entire sky for as far as we could see, using the vast Pacific Ocean as a palette. We joined the worshipers on the seawall, relishing the performance, and just when we thought we had experienced the most incredible colors imaginable, Mother Nature said, "You ain't seen nothing yet." And a whole new sequence of shamelessly extravagant bursts of colors would begin. It seemed to go on for a full forty-five minutes. There was even applause and cheers at several points during the show.

What I learned later was that Maui sunsets are like a religious experience. When an extraordinarily beautiful sunset happens, everyone stops and takes a deep breath to enjoy and appreciate one of the wonders of the world: the Maui Sunset.

We had arrived at the beginning of one of these spectacular events, and Maui folks were migrating to the seawall in states of mindfulness for that peaceful time in the day when the hubbub of the daytime segues into dusk and then night, when Mother Maui and all her inhabitants pause for a moment to take a deep, calming breath. It is a moment for quiet reflection and appreciation for *āina* (the land), *moana* (the ocean), and Mother Maui (as the spirit of the island is called). This was my introduction to a lifestyle that would become natural for me.

Maui county at the time had a total population of 53,000, compared to 163,000 now. If you hiked up Lahaina-Luna and looked down upon Lahaina town, you could imagine it was the 1800s and the old whaling village it used to be. The Aloha spirit was infused in everyone and everything. Moments after my feet touched Maui soil, I felt more at home there than I'd ever felt anywhere else; it was like coming home to a place I'd never been before.

Our band, named US, was a tight, hard-hitting jazz and R&B band consisting of:

Kit Ebersbach, keyboards

Larry Hall, trumpet and flugelhorn

Jerry Eubank, sax and flute

Paul Chun, bass

Larry McFall, drums

Myself, lead vocals and percussion

Gary Wilson, later, on reeds

Nick's Fish Market was a five-star restaurant and nightclub unlike anything Maui had ever seen. Nick catered to the rich and famous; movie stars, famous musicians, and celebrities from all over the world came to enjoy the delectable cuisine and the atmosphere he offered.

The waiters and waitresses kept up on current events including politics, sports, and economics, and were able to converse fluently on any subject. They wore black tuxedos and could light a woman's cigarette in a nanosecond; in fact, by the time she got it to her lips there would be at least two, maybe three lighters flicked and ready. I even saw a waiter try to light a pencil by mistake. The service and the food were beyond five-star.

Performing at Nick's, I had the opportunity to meet and play with lots of famous musicians. Some of them had outsized personalities and the belief that their excrement was perfume-scented (I won't mention any names), but most of them, like Bonnie Raitt and Boz Scaggs, were regular folks with extraordinary talent who still maintained that down-home attitude toward others.

And then there was Stevie Wonder.

We were in the middle of a set when we heard that Stevie Wonder was in town and on his way to the club. Word spread around the island quickly, and before we knew it, half the island was at the door with the crowd overflowing out into the hall and down the stairs. He arrived wearing a white Aloha shirt and Bermuda shorts, accompanied by his entourage. A huge wave of electrifying energy preceded him—you could feel his presence before he hit the door. When he entered, we were playing his song "Boogie on Reggae Woman." He swayed to the music, his head bobbing back and forth to the beat; he wore that dazzling smile he's famous for. You knew you were in the presence of music royalty, someone who was special beyond anything most of us had ever experienced. He lit up the room.

He sat and listened to our band for a few songs, and I have to say I was more than a little bit intimidated to have him in the audience. To me he was the ultimate musician. Everything about music rolled into this one rocking and rolling blind dude. We finally took a break, and I went over to his table to welcome him. I shook his hand and said, "Pleased to meet you, Stevie."

He took my hand and said, "Man, you've got some strong Leo energy coming out of you, brother."

That stumped me, there was no way he could've known ahead of time that I was a Leo. On top of being a musical genius, was he psychic, too? I was trying to maintain my cool.

I fought the urge to gush over him and say something stupid like, "Wow—how did you know that Stevie?!" Instead, I said, "Yeah, man, you got that right," somehow managing to maintain my cool, 'cause you know how important that is!

I touched his arm and said, "Hey, man, if the feeling's right, come on up and do a few tunes."

He said, "Absolutely, brother. I'd be glad to."

We went back on stage, played a couple of songs, and then invited him up. He was led to the stage by a member of his entourage, and he sat and got himself situated at the keyboard.

At the time, Kit, our keyboard player, had an ARP 2600 synthesizer. It was one of the early synthesizers that had so many patch cords and programs that it looked like one of the old telephone operator stations you see in '50s movies. To program it, you had to plug the cords into their sockets in a precise manner, or you'd end up with static or gobbly gook.

Stevie Wonder had it reprogrammed in seconds, then turned to me and said, "So, what do you want to sing, brother?"

This took me by surprise, and I had to fight off another bout of gushiness. I had expected to play behind him, but here he was asking me what I wanted to sing!

I turned to him and said, "How about 'Genius' by Valerie Simpson?"

He said, "What key?"

Then he started in on a rendition of "Genius" like I'd never heard before and have not heard since. The music just burst from him like a fountain. He forced me out of my comfortable little bubble into vocal improvisation I hadn't known I could do. He was one with the keyboards, one with the music; he was music personified, beyond words. He swept me and everyone in the club into his vortex.

I finally turned to him and said, Hey man, I'm gonna sit down and let you have the stage."

He said, "No problem, brother—here I go."

Then he broke into "Superstition," but not the "Superstition" you would hear on a CD or in concert. This was a funky, "I'm having fun here on Maui—and, oh, by the way, I'm gonna blow the roof off of this whole damn nightclub" version. His whole body rocked with the beat, his head rolling back and forth as if it had a life of its own—and of course there was that dazzling smile. The whole room was one electrifying point in space; it was like standing beneath Niagara Falls without a raincoat, or putting your finger in a five thousand-volt socket.

I was transfixed. I had been on stage with many famous musicians and in the presence of other important people, but none had exuded such captivating energy as Stevie Wonder. When he finally walked out the door, I turned to the band members and said, "How the hell do you follow something like that?"

We played at Nick's for nine months and then moved on to play at other clubs on Maui and other islands. We landed a gig at the Tradewinds on the big island of Hawaii, backing up a singer who thought he was James Brown but was always losing the key and having to ask me to hum the starting note. I think Kit was messing with him and intentionally giving him the wrong lead-in. Kit didn't have much patience with bozos and took it upon himself to try and drive them off the stage or drive them crazy—or a little of both.

We were staying at the Tradewinds Hotel. The Tradewinds was like a twenty-year-old car with a shine. It was almost nice but just a little off the mark; it had a single-level, Mid-Century design with rooms that surrounded a lush courtyard with palms, ferns, and other tropical vegetation. The bullet holes over the entrance should have given us an indication of what was to come.

One early morning we woke up to bright lights and bullhorns. The place was surrounded by police. It was a narcotics raid; turns out there was a major drug ring operating out of the place, and we just happened to be in the wrong place at the wrong time. One of the members of the band was holding a pretty good stash and got frantic until he realized we weren't under any scrutiny. But by then he had already flushed it down the toilet.

They closed the place down and we were out of a gig.

There was talk among the band members of heading to the mainland to play Vegas or some other big city venues. I said, "Sorry, but I think Maui is my home now." I had put down roots on the island and felt I had found my home. I had no desire to ever return to the mainland, much less live in a big city.

***

I was gradually making the transition from smooth-talking jazz musician to a Maui backwoods hippy. I exchanged my city slicker duds for cut-offs and tank tops, threw away my shoes, and moved into my van with a surfboard, diving gear, and my guitar. I'd take off hiking into the interior of the West Maui Mountains and stay for days at a time. I moved up into an old abandoned ranger's cabin in Poli Poli Park on the slopes of Haleakala, and that became home for a while. I'd dive for my food when I was near the ocean and harvest taro and other edible plants and shoot or trap pheasants, chukars, and doves for food when I was in the mountains.

I experienced Maui to the fullest. One of my favorite spots was the forest above the seven sacred pools located in Kipahulu on the Hana side of the island. I'd drive my van up through the cow pastures and camp at the foot of the mountains. There was a place just below the bamboo forest that most people didn't know about: the beginning of a magical water journey. It began with a thirty-foot dive off a beautiful waterfall into a deep pool. Once you took the dive there was really no way to get back up except to swim through a beautiful narrow canyon with inward-sloping walls and rivulets of water trickling over the sides, and then dive off several more waterfalls until you finally exited just before a spectacular hundred-foot waterfall. It was important to get out at the right spot unless you wanted to try an Evel Knievel over the falls. On a recent trip to Maui, I found they had blocked access to the canyon, probably for good reason.

I was hanging with my friend Lori a lot at the time. One of her friends, Kathy, was visiting from the mainland, so I decided to take them up to experience this swim. We dropped our clothes off at the take-out spot and proceeded up to the waterfall. Along the way we browsed on the magic mushrooms growing in abundance in the pasture. By the time we got to the waterfall, we had each consumed enough psilocybin that we could have floated there if we had wanted to. Back then, not many people came up that far, and no one could see over the edge of the waterfall, so we went au naturele.

We took the first dive into the pool, which was so clear you could see the bottom and the smooth rocks lying there. We swam a short forty feet or so to another precipice over which the stream cascaded with plumes of wispy spray held aloft by the up-canyon winds from below. Kathy and I jumped because we didn't know how deep the water was. When it was Lori's turn, she slipped on takeoff and bumped her way down the falls. Luckily, it wasn't a high fall, and she had enough padding that she wasn't injured.

From there we jumped from a couple of other minor waterfalls, then floated leisurely through a magical chasm stretching a hundred feet or so. The sky was a ribbon of blue, and thin runnels of water cascaded from the rocks above. Verdant ferns sprouted from every nook and cranny, and beautiful long vines of many varieties reached from the rim above to the water below. Sunlight filtering down through the lush greenery created thousands of glittering diamonds on the water's surface. It was a beautiful place to begin with, but by being enhanced by magic mushrooms, it was otherworldly. The colors were vivid, the waterfalls were slow-motion light shows, and the sunlight through the palms was electrifying; we could feel the crackling of the sun's energy in its rays, and the ferns and vines hanging from the cliffs were alive in a sentient kind of way.

According to legend, a grotto with a tunnel at the end led to a cave with a throne. Problem was that the tunnel was underwater, and you would have to hold your breath long enough to make it. I knew where it was, and I was a good swimmer, but I just wasn't ready to try, so we continued our leisurely swim until we climbed out at the pasture where my van was parked.

The pasture was riddled with depressions created by old collapsed lava tubes and on the way back down I managed to get my van stuck in one of these depressions. We were sitting there wondering how the hell we were going to get out when a tall Hawaiian *paniolo* (cowboy) riding a big white horse and wearing a ten-gallon hat (no joke!) came riding over the rise. I think he was stricken with Lori, so instead of chastising us for driving through the pasture, he pulled us out and let Lori go riding through the hills on his white horse, her long hair flowing in the wind and leaving colorful psychedelic trails in her wake. It was as if we were in a magical fairy tale that some long-haired, bearded, imaginative writer in a castle far away had written and chosen us for the main characters.

This character wasn't the same Ron who left Cincinnati over a gang fight—I was changing in more ways than you could imagine.

***

Growing up in Cincinnati, I felt like I had to do the inner-city version of being cool in order to fit in, but truthfully, I never really wanted to be cool. I went through the motions and did everything that was part of the culture, but it always felt kind of fake to me. There I had to maintain the image to keep people from messing with me.

There are certain phrases you were supposed to use, a certain way of talking, a certain way of walking, and if you did all these things, you were cool. Maybe some people believed the façade, but deep inside I knew it was just a front. It never felt comfortable to me—sort of like I was living someone else's version of me.

I carried this façade of "coolness" to Hawaii with me as it's a necessity to be cool if you are a jazz singer. I glided through life, maintaining my coolness to the nth degree. I began to believe the façade.

I was going through women like candy, thinking, "Oh, it's all right. I'm a musician." I was being insensitive and was approaching the realm of being a real jerk.... Okay, I pretty much was a jerk. Something had to change because I wasn't raised like that.

It came to a head one night when, after finishing a set, I sat next to a good friend of mine who turned to me and said, "You sound like shit tonight, Ron. You're not even trying."

At first, I was offended, but after thinking about it, I had to admit that she was right. I was just going through the motions, treading water, and occupying space. I was expecting people to accept whatever I put out. She didn't realize it, but her statement forced me to examine who I had become. Something was missing in my life.

Little by little, I was giving up who I was and becoming something different—what that was, I didn't know. They say you are a different person every day, and that was true for me. I found myself examining all the "truisms" that had guided me through life up to that point. I had studied some anthropology, psychology, and sociology in college. I understood that most social mores, laws, and religions are derived from the need to create a set of rules that allow us humans to live together, and that these rules became necessary once we moved from the family units to clans, tribes, mega-tribes, and finally the nations that we find ourselves in now. A level of manipulation is required to get the masses to function in a reasonable manner.

I also understood most of these systems were created for the good of all, but many of them were created by the reigning few just to keep the masses in check. Religion was one of the tools used, and they found it necessary to give promises of things like heaven, eternity, or seventy-two virgins for those who behave, and conversely to also have some form of punishment for those of us who didn't. The penance could be anything from a whack upside the head to damnation in Hell with the prospect of existing eternally in a perverse world of fire ruled by the devil.

At one point I gave up the belief of God and became agnostic. I believed that if there was a God, she wouldn't allow the suffering and pain I saw in the world. I couldn't believe she could turn a blind eye to the prejudice and cruelty humans are able to inflict on each other. I know a lot of people say things like "It's God's will" and "Everything God does is perfect" and rote statements like that. I wasn't buying it. To me, these sayings were just cop-outs and excuses that let people not take responsibility for what was happening or take actions to make change.

After some introspection I realized it was not God that I didn't believe in; it had more to do with religion and how people used it to suit their own needs. I was having trouble with the human manifestations of God and what they did in God's name.

Christianity has a vision of Jesus as this blond-haired, sharp-featured Anglo-Saxon-looking person who was sent here to Earth to save us from ourselves. His dad is often depicted as a white-haired, Anglo-Saxon who is watching over us and doling out goodness to those of us who follow the rules closely, while also inflicting pain and suffering in this world and the hereafter to those who don't. That was a myth that just did not work for me.

I was swimming and had lost my ground. I had to go back and examine everything I had learned in the Bible and in Buddhism, Taoism, Islam, and all the religions and manifestations of God I had been exposed to. I had to go back and explore who I had been and how I got to be what I was.

I had to do a reboot.

Chapter 24

WAIKAPU VALLEY

Learn in the Valley

"*I WENT TO THE woods because I wished to live deliberately, to front only the essential facts of life, and to see if I could not learn what it had to teach, and not, when I came to die, discover that I had not lived.*"——**Henry David Thoreau, *Walden***

"*We must become so alone, so utterly alone, that we withdraw into our innermost self. It is a way of bitter suffering. But then our solitude is overcome. We are no longer alone, for we find that our innermost self is the spirit, that it is God, the indivisible. And suddenly we find ourselves in the midst of the world, yet undisturbed by its multiplicity, for our innermost soul we know ourselves to be one with all being.*"
——**Hermann Hesse**

According to ancient Hawaiian lore, there was once an enchanted conch shell (*pu*) hidden in the valley of Waikapu and concealed deep within a lava tube that stretched from one end of the island to the other. When blown, the sound of this shell could be heard for miles. So compelling was this pu that a *kahuna* (Hawaiian witch doctor) from Kauai came to Maui in pursuit of it. But a mischievous dog by the name of Puapualenalena, a trickster in Hawaiian folklore, grabbed the conch first, whisked it away, and silenced the shell forever.

Waikapu valley was also the site of one of the greatest battles in Hawaiian history. Kalaniopuu, king of the big island, invaded Maui in an attempt to overthrow Kahelili, the Maui king. Kahelili's force annihilated Kalaniopuu's forces, killing thousands of warriors. It was said that the stream ran red with blood. Many people believe the spirits of these warriors still inhabit Waikapu Valley. There was a dark cloud that hung over the mouth of the valley, giving it a foreboding feel. Not many people ventured into that valley, but this is where I found myself.

Waikapu Valley is a deep verdant gash in the West Maui Mountains, the next major valley down from Iao Valley. In the valley, the only sounds were the wind blowing through the trees, doves cooing, and the tumbling stream that ran the length of the valley. The valley floor was adorned with kukui nut trees, koa, palms, and the occasional banana tree. The valley was my own Garden of Eden, and I had it pretty much all to myself.

Because of the remoteness of the valley, the sky was free from pollution of man-made light sources. This—along with the black lava rock, which absorbs any light—made for some spectacular light shows. At night, the stars were brighter and more distinct than I'd ever seen, except in Haleakala Crater. The clear stream ran the length of the valley, over rocks the size of cars that had been rounded by centuries of water erosion, with occasional blue-green pools. I drank freely from the waters until one day I discovered a half-eaten wild boar lying in the stream.

I had retreated into Waikapu Valley because I needed a "redo." I was at a point in my life where I wasn't happy with whom I had become. I had developed the attitude I had always detested in others, an attitude that, no matter what I did, it was okay because I was an artist. It had crept up on me over time through people loading me up with compliments, having had a recording contract, and rubbing elbows with the rich and famous—even though I was not one of them. It's something that seeps into your soul, and before you know it—poof, you're an asshole.

Well, I wasn't really an asshole, but I knew I needed to make a change and felt I couldn't do it while in the company of others. I had been gliding through life on the crest of a wave, propelled along by my voice, my personality, and the people supporting me. My experience has been that when you are riding the wave, you don't really feel the need to dig deep, to listen, to learn; but when you're in the trough, the valley between the waves, and have to find a way back to the crest, that is where the learning takes place.

So, I removed myself from society.

I took a tarp, an old army blanket, a machete, a .22 rifle, and some basic cooking utensils, and went to live in the valley. I also took the *Tao Te Ching*, *The Prophet* by Kahlil Jibran, the Bible, and Carlos Castaneda's books, *A Yaqui Way of Knowledge* and *A Separate Reality and Tales of Power*.

Being alone was one of the most difficult things I had ever done. When you're out in the world around other people, there are endless distractions: parties, conversations with friends, parties, keeping up with current events, TV, and more parties. Most of us never have an opportunity to spend extended time alone even if we want to, so we never have to—or even think to—face our inner selves, but this is what I went into the valley to do.

All the bravado and false pretenses we surround ourselves with in our lives as protection didn't work up there. It was a period of contraction for me, and little by little all the crutches fell away and became meaningless until it was down to just me. I felt like Smeagol in *The Lord of the Rings* who squirms, wriggles, makes excuses, begs, and threatens...until finally it's obvious none of that is going to work. Only then does the truth start coming out. You can't lie to yourself for very long and keep believing it—unless you have a nut loose.

All the little things I'd done in my life and had rationalized came back to me one by one, and one by one I had to examine them, accept what was okay, and deal with the rest. There were no friends to say, "Oh, that's cool, man." There was no one there to try and convince me everything was okay even when I knew it wasn't. I was like a snake shedding its old skin, who for a time is raw, exposed, and vulnerable, and who then must begin the process of creating a new skin that will encapsulate the expanded being.

Waikapu Valley at night was a spooky place. The darkness was close to absolute, the light seemingly sucked away by a giant light vacuum; what light there was came from the stars shining like bright diamonds against a sea of darkness. Then there were the weird sounds you heard at night for which there was no explanation. It made you feel small, fragile, and exposed.

I spent nights gazing at the Milky Way and other constellations and galaxies. I spent my days contemplating my place in this world and my belief in God and evaluating all the concepts of God I had learned in church and other places. I wanted to connect with God, but I wanted a direct connection—not through an interpreter.

I read my books, looking for truths I could accept and discarding things I couldn't. Then I put the books away and began my process of rebuilding—the beginning of my rebirth.

I began meditating using the transcendental meditation techniques I had learned through Maharishi Mahesh Yogi's training. I meditated for hours, and sometimes for days, until I felt I was floating above the earth. I used the techniques Don Genaro had taught Carlos Castaneda, and I fasted for up to seven days at a time. I practiced astral projection, projecting myself over distances until I was successful enough that I almost didn't want to come back.

I experienced charges of light energy that were like plugging myself into a socket connected to everything that had ever been, all that was, and all that was to come. I surrendered every raw nerve ending to the universe and felt as though I pulsed with the beat of the earth, with the movement of the wind and the waves; I felt the slight undulations as the moon passed over, pulling at me like the tides. I began to understand the theory of entanglement—once things are connected, they are always energetically connected with everything in existence back to the beginning of time.

Sometimes when I came out of the valley for supplies people would look at me and recoil in shock, asking, "Man, what the hell are you on?" I must have looked scary. I had dreadlocks, was down to about 147 pounds, and had an otherworldly look in my eyes. I was dark from being in the sun so much, and my blue eyes stood out from my face like two crystals in a field of coal.

I had a system where I would do a one-day fast every Monday, a three-day fast once a month, and a seven-day fast once a year. At the end of the seven-day fast, I felt as if I could fly and had lost most of my desire to eat. I felt as if my mind was clear and my body was jamming along on eight cylinders. I realized how much time was spent on the acquisition and preparation of food and had to force myself to begin to eat again.

As most of us have at some point or other in our lives, I contemplated the infiniteness of it all.

To this day I struggle with a way to put into words what I connected to in the valley. Wise people from other cultures have described it as God, Gaia, Chi, or life energy; I was not presumptuous enough to give it a name, so for want of a better name, I'll call it God. It is the energy that allows a tiny redwood seed to become a massive three hundred-foot giant and live for centuries and the force that lets a baby come into this life fully formed and breathing. I felt the constant molecular movement we normally mistake as static in the rocks, in the trees, and in the earth. I pondered the process of things going from one state to another: energy to matter, matter to energy or whatever is between—and my own eventual return to pure energy.

I was enveloped by the most peaceful and serene feeling. There was no good or bad, no pain, no worries—just an absolute and overwhelming feeling of peace.

In the stillness of the valley I felt the souls of those who had come before us wafting in the breeze, blowing through the trees, and in the birds riding the wind. I could feel them in the flowers rising from the earth and the rocks and trees. They were with me in the morning and evening, in every breath I took.

I felt content with the idea that there was no end, just new beginnings.

When I'd first read the books and listened to the sermons, I found it hard to accept all those words at face value. I couldn't accept that those people were direct conduits to God. Maybe some of them were, but there were so many posers out there that I couldn't tell the bad from the good.

So, what it came down to is this: Was I going to accept there is a God? Is there a guiding hand in the creation of this small blue marble, the universe, and beyond?

I don't know exactly what God is, but I do know that God is. But for me, it's not the image of God most religions have felt the need to create. God is not dependent upon me to define it. God just is. The importance of understanding or defining what God is, is no longer with me.

I must revert back to verse one of the *Tao Te Ching*:

The Tao that can be told
is not the eternal Tao.
The name that can be named
is not the eternal name.
The Tao is both named and nameless.
As nameless it is the origin of all things;
As named it is the Mother of 10,000 things.
Ever desireless, one can see the mystery;
Ever desiring, one sees only the manifestations.
And the mystery itself is the doorway to all understanding.

—Translation by Jonathan Star and quoted by Dr. Wayne W. Dyer

(Note: 10,000 things is representative of worldly wants, needs, and possessions.)

When I came out of the valley, I was a transformed person, humbler and more comfortable with my place in this world. I had caught a glimpse of what it was like to connect with "God" for want of a better word, a pure and unadulterated connection to the divine source. That strength is what has gotten me through the rest of my life. Now I wake up every morning and say my gratitude's for the many things we are blessed with. I am thankful for my time in this form on earth.

Now I understand why many primitive societies incorporated rites of passages and spiritual journeys into their cultures that required them to travel into nature and find their own connection. I understand the reasons for the sweat lodges of the Plains Indians, the walkabouts of Australia's Aboriginals, and the warrior camps of the Maasai warriors. Sometimes I wonder if, by moving into a more civilized society, are we just taking someone else's pre-packaged view of what our connection with God should be, instead of exploring and accepting our own relationship?

I understand why, when we look into the eye of the elephant, we see the wisdom inherent in them, pure and unpolluted by the knowledge and abilities we've been blessed—or cursed—with. I see that they are dependent upon us to tap into the goodness of our Godliness and make the right decisions to continue our shared life on this earth.

Now when people ask if my glass is half full or half empty, I have to say, "My cup runneth over."

***

"Learn in the Valley, But Don't Live in it"

Before I went into the valley, in a conversation with a friend of mine who was purported to be clairvoyant, she said, "You have a propensity to become reclusive, maybe even a recluse, but don't worry because a beautiful maiden will rescue you from your seclusion." I didn't pay her much mind at the time.

In my first month out of the valley, I stopped by my friend Ward's place. Ward was a Maui institution. He had moved to Maui from

Berkeley, California, after becoming disillusioned during the last phases of his studies in philosophy. A tall Black dude with wild, curly hair; wide, flaring nostrils, and a generous spare tire, he always had a pencil stuck behind his ear or in his hair. He described his house as "the only ghetto in all of Maui." We simply called it "the Wailuku House."

The Wailuku house was actually three old plantation houses situated on one lot. The buildings were all old, broken-down shacks with chickens having the run of the place. The back house was used as a woodworking shop where Ward and his partner Nick made beautiful custom furniture and cabinets for island customers. The house next to it was where Ward and his family lived. It had a beautiful bougainvillea hedge with huge red blooms and one of the best butter avocado trees in Maui.

Then there was the big house. The Wailuku Big House was the crash pad for anyone coming to Maui who didn't have a place to stay. It had multiple rooms with a roof that had expired decades ago. Patched screens, no windows, no front door, and no locks—probably because there was nothing of value to steal, but also because there was not much crime in Maui back then. There was a series of tarps inside, arranged so when it rained, the tarps directed the water into little rivulets throughout the house and channeled it out the windows. The Big House looked like an old, beaten-down plantation house from the outside, but it was our communal monastery of sorts.

It was inhabited by a mixture of locals, *kamainas* (local word for mainlainders who had lived on the island for a long time), and people in transition, all inhabiting the same space. It was a place where everyone was in total acceptance of each other, mentally, physically, and spiritually. It was an oasis in time and space, existing for a brief period that served to connect and nurture us all.

One day, I was sitting on the back porch of the Big House, drinking beer with some local friends, when I saw a girl I had never seen before. Tall, tan with Hazel eyes and long brown hair with legs that gracefully reached from the ground to a perfectly shaped okole. She was planting flowers around the perimeter of the house. She was streaked with mud from digging in the dirt, and her hair was all askew, but she had a sparkle in her eyes and I could see that there was beauty beneath. My friend Sonny Swift was amazed someone was trying to beautify this old ghetto-looking place.

I said, "Hey, Sonny, who is that chick?"

He said, "Oh, that's Nancy. She just came over from the mainland."

I asked, "What the hell is she doing?"

Sonny took a swig of his Primo beer and said, "Eh, brodda, no ask me. She must be *pupule* (crazy) or something!"

We sat there drinking our cheap beer, watching this pretty mainland girl trying to beautify this ghetto-looking place, and wondered what her motivations were. No one had ever taken it upon themselves to try and change this place; we all just accepted it the way it was. This was something new. I kinda liked it—and her!

A few days later, I had a couple of tickets to a Beamer Brothers concert, a Hawaiian singing group, and I offered to take Nancy. She accepted. Sitting there listening to the smooth, lilting voices of the Beamers, we realized we both had a love and appreciation of Hawaiian music with its melodic, laid-back island style. This was just one of many things we discovered we had in common. The next day I showed her around the island because it was her last day on Maui and I realized she had not had the opportunity to see the sights. Then the day after, she left for San Francisco and a job she had been offered.

I assumed that was the end of it, but a couple of weeks later Ward stopped me and said, "Hey, you remember that girl you took to the Beamer Brothers concert? She wants you to call her."

She had called Ward because he was the only person in our group who had a phone.

When I called her back, she said, "Would you consider coming to live with me in San Francisco? I'm feeling kind of lonely and would love to have you here with me."

Well, at the time I was an island boy and had no intention of ever leaving the island, but I found myself saying, "Give me a couple weeks, and I'll be there."

When I told my friends, they were totally amazed. The thought of me dropping everything and moving to the mainland to be with a woman I had just met was like believing it would snow in Waikiki. But I saw something in her, and she obviously saw something in me—I still don't know what it was, I was broke, unemployed and with no prospects or desire for employment.

I sold most of my worldly possessions (though there weren't many), packed my bags, and hopped a plane to the Bay Area. We rented a basement flat in a three-level house in San Anselmo, where

I was reminded I was back on the mainland when, while taking a walk around the neighborhood, a police car pulled in front of me and blocked my path. The officer inquired if I had business in the neighborhood. In other words, "What the hell is your Black ass doing in this lily-white neighborhood?"

I replied, "I live here, Officer," and pointed to my house.

He looked at me like I was crazy, shook his head, backed up, and drove away. Welcome back to the mainland!

We lived in San Anselmo for a while, then Berkeley, and then we decided to take off and explore the Pacific Northwest. We bought an old beater Buick station wagon, a timeworn surplus canvas army tent, and other camping supplies, and we hit the road. We traveled up through northern California, passing through Willits and Ukiah, marveling at the majestic redwoods and enjoying the beautiful Northern California coast. We wound our way up through the Pacific Northwest and found ourselves at an almost deserted campground in Oregon on the shore of Lake Billy Chinook. We camped there for three weeks. At the time, Oregon hadn't been discovered by the masses, and we were pretty much the only campers for the entire time.

Nancy had lived in Idaho for a while before coming to Hawaii, so we next headed east to Idaho. One of our first stops was a natural hot spring Nancy knew about. We followed a faint trail through a patch of woods and a series of beautiful meadows before finally coming to a steaming depression along a creek, just large enough for the two of us. We disrobed and eased into the soothing hot water. We weren't paying much attention to our surroundings, just enjoying each other and nature, when we heard someone approach and ask, "Are you decent?" It was an older couple who must've frequented the spring.

Nancy turned and said, "Yes, we're decent!"

They walked up to the pool and, seeing we were in fact buck naked, turned and left.

I asked Nancy, "Why'd you tell them we were decent when we're naked?"

She looked at me and said, "Well, we are decent people!"

I laughed. "Okay, you got me there!"

Forty- five years later, we're still together, and she keeps our deck, our surrounding property, and our lives constantly in bloom, just as she did the first day I saw her.

If I had met her before going into the valley, I don't know if she would have wanted to hang out with me, and I wouldn't have been worthy of someone like her. It was as if I had to spend time in the valley, clearing out all the old bad shit, so I could be ready for her.

We eventually moved back to Maui, where we were married in Iao Valley. Iao Valley is a lush valley in the West Maui mountains that had a distinctive sharp projection rising from the valley floor that locals called "The Needle." Guava trees and palms adorned the sides of the valley, and a wide, tumbling creek ran its length. It was an island wedding, and we put it out in the Maui grapevine, saying, "Hey, Ron and Nancy are getting married. Come help us celebrate!" People from all over the island descended upon Iao Valley for the celebration. Two large ponds stocked with colorful Koi occupied the middle of the lower part of the valley, with a small bridge spanning the two sides. This was where we were married.

Afterward, our friend David McClellan commented, "I wondered where all the flower children went when they left Woodstock—they all came here!"

Of note was the absence of either of our families: mine for financial reasons, and Nancy's partially for racial ones. Her mom, having been enveloped by the racially monoethnic society of Dearborn, Michigan, for most of her life, could not accept that a person of African descent was piercing the sanctity of her White family. This was a quandary many families were having to deal with as young people realized that the taboos of racial mixing had no basis and the fallacies past generations had adopted were not acceptable to them.

For years afterward, she could not bring herself to accept her Black son-in-law or even her mixed grandchildren. While Nancy's Father and her sisters ventured out to meet us and spend time with us, she would not, could not. When we went back to visit, we noticed photos of other grandchildren, nieces, nephews, and even neighborhood kids, but no pictures of our children.

I'm sure it was a source of considerable heartache for Nancy, but she dealt with it in an honorable manner. She finally expressed her exasperation in a letter to her mom, letting her know she was missing out on getting to know her family and watching her grandchildren grow up. I wish I could have witnessed the soul-searching her mom went through, but after years of denial, she finally came around and wholeheartedly embraced me and the kids in a grand and gracious manner.

She made regular visits to Oregon and welcomed us to Dearborn, making a point to introduce us to her closest friends, unabashed, unashamed and in fact enormously proud of her daughter's family. When I was convalescing from a neck injury, she was the one who took the time to write weekly letters of encouragement. I often wonder what took her over the edge from abject denial to complete acceptance. If I knew, I would put it in aerosol cans, rent an airplane, and spray it all over the world.

At one point during one of our visits to Dearborn, I pulled her aside and complimented her for her courage in overcoming the myths she had been burdened with for her entire life. She of course thanked us for helping her see the other side of things, and then she gave me a hug and told me how much she loved me and my family.

That was a good day.

Chapter 25

Pacific Northwest

A FTER LIVING ON THE islands for fourteen years, we finally got Rock Fever, which is what Island folks call the sense of confinement that comes from living on a rock in the middle of the ocean for an extended period of time. I mean, you can only go around the island so many times and not get tired of it. I had explored the interior of the island, surfed, scuba dived, fished, and done all the things you do on an island. I had tried to get through college several times, but when the surf was up or the fishing good, it was hard to concentrate on studies.

As much as I loved the islands, it was time to move on.

We decided Nancy would stay on Maui and work while I went to the mainland to look for a new home for us. So, I jumped on a jet plane and headed east.

I landed in Berkeley, California, where I stayed with a good friend while I gathered supplies and information about towns in California, Oregon, and Alaska. I bought a four-wheel-drive truck and headed north.

I was naive about how things really were in the Pacific Northwest and didn't know what to expect. Lots of folks are still ignorant about the Northwest portion of the country. I had one friend ask, "Aren't you worried about the Indians out there?" Another asked, "Do they have electricity and stuff?" Conversely, I found that lots of Northwest folks were, and still are, ignorant about Black folks.

I wound my way up through northern California, stopping to visit small towns we had researched, branching off to explore the backroads, and experiencing the majestic Douglas firs, redwoods, and cedars that seemed to reach to the sky. I marveled at the crystal-clear rivers of the Pacific Northwest and the pristine blue alpine lakes. I saw bald eagles, deer, and elk. I caught rainbow trout and cooked them over a campfire. I sat and contemplated the overwhelming expanse of tall fir trees stretching for as far as I could see and understood why the early loggers thought there was a never-ending supply of trees.

I looped over into Idaho for a short time before realizing that, although the Sawtooth Mountains were some of the most beautiful mountains in existence, Idaho was not for me.

Everyone has a story, and you can learn so much just by listening to people. I made a habit of meeting people in campgrounds and listening to their opinions of places and things. One night I was at a campground in southern Oregon, sitting around a crackling campfire with an older gentleman from Grants Pass, Oregon, and a couple of other campers. I told him I was thinking about moving to Oregon and was looking for a nice town to settle down in. I asked, "Are there many Black folks in Grants Pass?"

He got a puzzled look on his face and said, "Let me go ask my wife."

He left and came back in a bit and said, "She said she thinks she saw one walking down the street a couple of years ago, but never saw him again."

I decided Grants Pass probably wasn't for me, so I headed north.

I finally stopped in Eugene, Oregon town for gas and engaged in a conversation with the gas station attendant about music. When he learned I was a musician he said, "You should go down to Jo Federico's and check it out."

I decided to take him up on it.

That night, I went to the club. Descending a flight of unassuming stairs, I entered through a thick oak door to arrive in a jamming, smoke-filled basement bar. Bass player Andre St. James and a lively jazz quartet were playing that night. When I walked in, they were in the middle of "Green Dolphin Street," a jazz standard that happened to be one of my favorites. They were playing to an audience of attentive jazz enthusiasts who were paying rapt attention to the music, except for the bartender, who was busy showing one of the customers her new tits. I thought, "Okay, I'm feeling at home here already. There's a good jazz scene here, and people are not too up-tight, so that's a good sign."

I grabbed a seat toward the back of the room, close enough to hear but not close enough to be noticed. Andre was a tall, dark, distinguished-looking gentleman dressed neatly in all black except for a white tie. He was thoroughly involved in the composition but took the time to give me a nod. I think he must have had the sixth sense some jazz folks have that informs us of when we are around one of our own kind. Shortly after, the band took a break, and I had a chance to talk with the them and some of the patrons. It all felt good—comfortable.

I spent the night sleeping in the back of my truck, got up the next day, and started walking around town. Everyone I met gave me a big smile and said hello. After talking with folks that I met, one of the things I noticed was that most of them were originally from somewhere else. I got the feeling Oregon was one of the furthest points west for the black sheep of other towns and families to go to, and I was definitely one of those.

I met folks from Midwest towns who just hadn't fit in with their former neighbors because of political leanings, people from the South who were raised in religious households but didn't share their families' beliefs, people from southern California who were trying to escape the city sprawl, and folks who had just succumbed to the urge to head west.

And me? I was just trying to find a place where Nancy and I could settle and maybe raise children someday. The longer I stayed, the more comfortable I felt.

Finally, I called her and said, "I think I've found us a new home." She said, "Yay! I'll start packing!"

I flew back to Maui and collected Nancy, and together we moved to Oregon. We got there the day Mount St. Helens blew her top. We woke up that morning with ash blanketing our car and the sun darkened with ash. It was a Pacific Northwest welcome!

Chapter 26

RANGER RON

I've always had an affinity for the outdoors. My sisters thought I was a strange kid. My oldest sister, in trying to describe her son to me, said, "He's kinda weird. You know, like you were, always out in the woods chasing rabbits or by the pond catching tadpoles—weird things like that!"

There wasn't a whole lot of nature to experience around the hood where I grew up except for a patch of woods by the railroad tracks, but I read books about the great outdoors, like Jack London's *Call of the Wild* and *White Fang*. So, when I got to Oregon and saw the huge expanses of trees, with beautiful clear rivers winding their way through the deep valleys, and the pristine mountain lakes, I decided I was going to live out my dream and become a forest ranger—you know, Ranger Ron!

I applied for a job with the U.S. Forest Service, and after a series of interviews I was hired to work as a forestry technician and tanker driver for wildland forest fires. On the first day, I walked into the ranger station and said, "Oh, yes, and by the way, I'm also a tree feller."

They probably knew I was lying because I didn't even pronounce it right—it's spelled "feller," but they call them tree fallers, not fellers. But that's what I wanted to do, and I was doing the old "fake it 'til you make it" thing. They probably got a good laugh about it but figured, *If he's got balls enough to do it, let him have at it!*

I went to the library and read every book they had about felling timber and the methods, dangers, and life expectancy of a timber feller. I found that loggers are injured or killed at a rate thirty times greater than that of any other profession. There are many things that can go wrong: a gust of wind could blow at the wrong time and send the tree back on you; a tree might hit other trees' branches on its way down and send a widowmaker your way; a slab of bark or a branch may become dislodged and come down on you. I've even seen trees hit a stump a hundred feet out and come straight back at you. They move much faster than you would think, and you have little time to get out of the way.

I had handled a chainsaw before and was familiar with the basics, so I practiced—mostly on the job—and after some time, I became good at taking down the massive Douglas firs when needed. When there were fires, I took down trees with burning tops that had been struck by lightning or had been ignited by flying sparks. I'd have a watcher with a long stick stand back and tap me on the back when something was coming down from the top so that I could drop the saw and run. I once took down a six-foot-diameter fir on a steep slope with a burning top. With a bandanna covering my nose and occasionally coughing because of the thick smoke, it took me over an hour to do it, but I put it exactly where I wanted it. I think about doing things like that now and shudder. I must have had an industrial-strength guardian angel looking after me.

I worked in Oakridge, Oregon—a little logging town in Western Oregon. Its claim to fame is that the movie *The Monster from the Green Lagoon* was filmed there. In 1980 Oakridge was a thriving town with a mixture of mill workers, loggers (they call them loggers, not lumberjacks), and forest service workers. The smell of freshly cut firs was always present, and log trucks almost outnumbered cars.

Oakridge lies in the foothills of the Cascade mountain range, which divides eastern Oregon from western Oregon. The city is near where the mighty Willamette River's headwaters are located. The Cascades serve as a sail to catch the water-laden ocean winds that, in turn, deposit moisture in the form of rain and snow on the western slopes. The result is miles of verdant forests, rich ferns, rhododendrons, and berries of all kinds. The Cascades are also home to the stately Douglas fir forests, which seem to go on forever.

At one point I realized I was probably the only Black person for fifty or so miles in either direction, but that was okay. I did a lot of educating.

When my supervisors were trying to decide who was going to train me on the fire tankers, they said, "Well, if we put him with Carl, he'll probably talk his ear off. Or we could put him with Bob Priest, but he might not even talk to him."

Bob was, from all appearances, the ultimate redneck: a big, six-foot-tall, bow-legged dude who drove a jacked-up black Ford truck with the ever-present rifle in the back window. He wore a wide-brimmed cowboy hat and a massive rodeo belt buckle. He even talked with a drawl between copious chews of snuff.

I said, "Put me with Priest."

What they didn't know was that Priest was the king of practical jokes, and I was a runner up. We got along so well that we became a tag-team. Our practical joking got bad enough that people would run when they saw the two of us coming because they knew we were up to no good. We became best of friends.

We had an old Douglas fir log behind the forest service warehouse we used for testing our chainsaws before going out on a fire. I was walking by one day and noticed Lawson, a rugged second- or third-generation woodsman and son of a logger. He was someone who prided himself on keeping his chainsaw sharp and in tip-top shape, and he was standing there with a puzzled look on his face. He was doing a test cut on the old log, but try as he might, the chain wasn't biting. He turned the saw off, inspected the chain, started it again, and engaged the log—with the same result.

Then I looked over at Bob, who was sitting on a log about to bust his britches laughing. Larson saw me looking at Bob, cut off his saw, walked over to Bob, and said, "Okay, you son of a bitch, what did you do to my saw?"

While Lawson had been in the bathroom, Bob had taken the saw apart, turned the chain around backwards, and then put it back together. Who the hell else would think about doing something like that! Bob had a warped mind.

Once, his daughter Robbi went on a date to town with one of the local Oakridge guys. Robbi, just like her mom and dad, didn't take shit from anybody and didn't have a problem letting folks know what she was thinking. On the way back to Oakridge after their date, as they drove past my house, her date pointed and said, "There's a nigger living there."

Without missing a beat, she said, "Oh, yeah, that's my dad's best friend."

Afterward, she told her dad, "He kinda shrank up within himself and didn't talk for the rest of the drive home!"

The next day Bob told me what had happened, and we rolled on the ground laughing. I laughed so hard I thought I was gonna die!

Bob Priest was one of the most unforgettable characters in my life and a true outdoorsman. He knew the Northwest territory like the back of his hand and could name every mountain, river, creek, and draw. He could tell you where to fish or hunt to be successful and could handle a gun like it was an extension of his arm. He'd catch fish when nobody else could. I'd go fishing with Bob and catch maybe five fish; Bob would catch fifteen. While everyone else was still out trying to fill an elk tag, Bob would have gotten his elk, dressed it, and sat back to drink a beer.

If you asked how to get to some hidden lake no one else knew about, he'd tell you how to get there and what time the fish started biting and say, "But watch out for that tree stump halfway down the bank. Don't trip on it." When you got there, there would be the tree stump!

When I first started, I'm sure it was obvious to him that I was a greenhorn. Sure, I had pretty much lived off the land for a time in Hawaii, but the Pacific Northwest with its massive trees and vast wilderness areas was another story and about ten steps above anything I had ever experienced. Bob taught me about the Oregon territory and the lay of the land. He taught me how to fish for landlocked salmon (*kokanee*), rainbow trout, and steelhead. He gave me the lowdown on hunting and showed me all the little tricks that help you get by out in the woods. He did all of this without letting on that he knew what a rookie I was.

Twenty years later I went to Bob and his wife Linda's fiftieth wedding anniversary celebration and saw some of the Oakridge folks I used to work with. Turns out they had all been following my progress in the business world since I had left Oakridge; one of them even had newspaper and magazine clippings from articles I had been featured in. I realized that I was still an Oakridge boy as far as they were concerned.

Bob and I remain good friends to this day. To quote a tired cliché, "you really can't judge a book by its cover," and you could miss out on what could be some of your best experiences in your life if you do.

***

In Oakridge, I spent a lot of time educating people about race, gender, and other things. Once a year we had a trainer who would come down from the main office and test the tanker drivers. The test consisted of taking the tanker out on the narrow, winding forest service roads, where we had to negotiate the twists and turns and avoid getting run off the road by the big log trucks that ran the same roads.

I was out with one trainer when the conversation turned to race. He asked if my wife was White.

I said, "Why, yes, she just happens to be White. Why do you ask?"

He said, "I don't have a problem with that. I just feel sorry for the kids."

I didn't say a word.

At the next opportunity to turn off the main road, I turned up into a little side road, stopped the truck, and said, "Get out, and let's talk."

I took off my sunglasses and said, "What color are my eyes?"

He said, "They're blue." And then he realized what that meant. He had just invalidated my very existence.

I said, "So, it's okay to discriminate against Black kids as long as they're all Black, but when they get White blood in them, then you feel sorry for them?"

Then we sat on a log and had a long conversation about race relations: what's true and what's not; what's okay and what's not; and the difference between fact and things that just pop out of your mouth because you've heard other people say them enough times that they just become the thoughtless things to say. In other words, we had a "Come to Jesus" talk.

At the end of our conversation, he apologized and said, "I guess I should think about the meaning of my words before I say them."

He was actually a nice guy but had always listened to his right-wing conservative talk show hosts, read only conservative newspapers, and was surrounded by people repeating things they had heard from talk show liars and truth-stretchers. Since no one ever challenged them, those words became truth to them.

I've had people want to tell me nigger jokes and think it was okay. I'd stop them and ask, "What makes you think I would want to hear a joke making fun of my race?"

I was like an ambassador and the encyclopedia of race. For many of them I was the only chance they'd ever had to interact with an African American person, and they had to take the opportunity to ask questions. They had been operating in a vacuum. There was a dearth of reliable information about Black people, and I was their opportunity to learn.

What I realized after a while was that most of these people were good folks in their own way. They were incredibly smart people and had the country common sense many of city folk lack. But, living in a small mountain town, they also had a lot of misinformation about other races and cultures. Things they saw on TV, that they heard on the news, or that got passed around between them had become truth. Well, I guess I was elected to enlighten them.

It was not just Black folks they were misinformed about but also women and other minorities. We were on our way back from a fire once and passed a work group of Hispanic tree planters. One of the guys in the truck said, "Look at the beaners out there in the field."

I stopped the van, backed up to where the work crew was, and said, "Okay, let's go out there and ask them how they feel about being called 'beaners.'"

He said, "Oh, man, I didn't mean anything by that!"

I told him, "Well, don't say something about someone they wouldn't appreciate hearing in person."

Same with lewd comments about women; I came around a corner once and heard the last part of a lewd conversation about one of the female crew members. One of the guys said, "Man, you better not let Ron hear you say that!" I guessed I had gained a reputation.

Sometimes, though, I'd see things that weren't there. Standing in line in a grocery store, I noticed a guy across the aisle staring at me. I got out of line, walked over to him, and asked, "Is there a problem?"

He said, "Oh, I'm sorry, man; I was just looking at your eyes. You've got some really cool eyes!"

I had to backtrack; I stood there kicking the ground a bit and thanked him for the compliment. After enough similar situations, I realized that sometimes I was projecting issues onto people that were not there; I had to "check myself." Now, I assume the best, and if it turns out to be not so, I'll deal with it if it's worth my time. Otherwise —I'll let it go past like a wind that blows and is gone.

I also realized most of these country folks would treat you with the utmost respect if you earned it—no matter what your color. They would defend you to the death if they liked you, but if they didn't—well, you might as well move. If you acted like an asshole, they would treat you like an asshole—and in their opinion, assholes came in all colors.

I remembered reading somewhere that most racism is a byprod-
uct of ignorance or misinformation. The more I worked in rural
areas, the more I believed that. Of course, there are some people who
are just jerks, and they would probably be jerks no matter what color
they are. With those types of people, you might just have to wait for
them to die and hope they haven't passed their poison onto their
kids or others.

Chapter 27

FIRE

WORKING FOR THE FOREST service was one of my dreams come true. We fought fires in some of the most remote and rugged country in Oregon, Idaho, Oregon, and California and even as far east as Kentucky and Tennessee. Sometimes they would drop us off by chopper on a remote ridge to fight a fire in the area and just leave us there. At night when the fire died down, we'd drop down into the canyons and low country and work to create a buffer for fire breaks, then relax on the ridgetop during the day.

We were on a massive fire in the Sierra Nevada range of California, taking a break after climbing up a steep talus slope, when Jackson, one of the crew members, glared at Priest and said, "You son of a bitch. I know it was you!" He pulled a grapefruit-sized rock from his pack. "I was wondering why I was having such a hard time coming up that hill!"

Bob had placed the rock in Jackson's pack back in Oregon some-where, all the way at the bottom of the pack where he knew Jackson wouldn't notice it. Jackson was normally like the Eveready rabbit:

light on his feet and at the head of the line. But we had noticed he had been getting slower and slower. His get-up-and-go had got up and went, and he had had a perplexed look on his face, wondering what the hell was happening to him.

"Hey, man, don't look at me. I don't know how that rock got in your pack," Priest said with a straight face. He was the world's greatest liar.

We flew from the California fire to a big fire in Idaho. The back and forth bantering and practical jokes had been continuous throughout the plane ride from California to the airport and had continued in the bus transporting us to the fire camp.

As we drew closer, the unmistakable smell of a big forest fire filled the air. It's different from the smell of a structure fire; it's a sinister, thick, ominous smell that carries with it a sense of something foreboding.

The closer we got, the less talking; the joking stopped, and there was mixture of excitement and dread permeating the once jovial mood. I looked around and saw that everyone had the same serious look that comes from facing something much larger than you. I'd seen that look on the faces of big wave surfers at Waimea Bay when the big surf came in. It's the realization that, although you may temporarily be on top, any victory you may have is temporary and could turn into disaster in a heartbeat.

From the air, we had seen the devastation this fire was wreaking. We got to fire camp and exited the van. Out came the bandannas to try and minimize the smoke damage to our lungs, although we all knew this was just the beginning—the worst was yet to come when we got out on the fire line. Ash covered everything, and even though it was mid-day, it felt like dusk. The diffused light from the smoke and ash in the air created an ethereal muted orange hue that seemed unworldly. The overall effect was sobering.

The helicopter arrived to take us to the fire line. The Bell Ranger, used by the forest service because of its reliable nature, was loud and kicking up dust; we boarded, and it took us six at a time to a remote ridgetop. We saw the fire below like something alive: a twisting, reaching dragon that created its own weather and basically went wherever the hell it wanted.

"Try and stop me—I dare you," it seemed to say.

At dusk, there was a moment of stillness as the hot up-canyon winds and cooler down-canyon drafts met at the top of the ridge, and a temporary stalemate was reached. Then the night descended upon us and the cooler down-canyon winds moved in and began to calm the dragon below. This was when we grabbed our chainsaws, shovels, and Pulaski's and descended into the canyon to try and slow its advance, or at least remove some of the fuel it feasted upon.

There was no talk except for the occasional shout of "rock" or "heads up!," and then everyone would stop and look up and around to make sure they weren't in the path of whatever was coming down. Randy Wells led the way. Randy, a tall, athletic Lakota Sioux from the Dakotas, seemed to be part owl and part wolf—he could see in the dark and run for hours. I operated the chainsaw, taking out the big stuff. I was followed by the swamper, who moved the big stuff from the fire trail we were creating. The remainder of the crew chopped, dug, and grubbed their way through the brush and trees until, when the last person passed, there was a perfectly clean, three-foot-wide path clear of all flammable material. This was our weapon, our attempt to stop the advance of the beast. Somehow it seemed feeble after seeing what we were working against.

We worked through the night. I looked around and saw faces streaked with ash from the fire, faces sometimes close to exhaustion but with the knowing look of, "Ain't nobody gonna carry your ass up out of this canyon. You got yourself down here, and you're gonna have to climb out by your own damn self."

Halfway through the night we stopped for a break, sitting on a rock ledge overlooking the canyon below. We could see the flicker of the fire on the other side of the canyon, but since it was so far away and on the other side of the river, we felt it was no danger to us.

The dragon was not dead, though, only sleeping. Suddenly the fire made a huge surge up the other side of the canyon, consuming everything in its path. The sound was like a thousand freight trains, the sky was lit up like high noon, and the fire went from the bottom of the canyon to the ridgetop in a matter of seconds. We sat there in awe, mesmerized by what we were seeing, the orange light reflecting on our faces like a solar flare.

Finally, Lisa broke the spell and said, "You know, if it did it on that side, it could do it on this side, too."

Then the wind shifted, and we were hit with an overpowering blanket of thick, pungent smoke. We grabbed for our bandannas and covered our mouths and noses to try and keep from inhaling the acrid smoke. Someone started coughing—a deep hacking sound like their lungs were trying to rid themselves of something foul.

There was a pause as we contemplated what Lisa had just said. Then almost in unison everyone was on their feet, moving away—walking, walking faster, then running up and away from the fire. I looked around and saw that a couple of the new people on the crew were close to panicking. I dropped back and told some of the other more seasoned members to keep an eye on them, since we didn't want them to get separated from the crew. I've seen people get disoriented in the smoke and almost run right into the fire.

We finally reached our safe place: an area of black charred ground that had already burned over and where there was no fuel left to burn. Everyone collapsed on the ground, exhausted.

Then someone started laughing. "Man, you should have seen the look on your face! You were scared shitless!"

"Oh, fuck you, man. Like you weren't scared."

"Shit no, I wasn't scared, I was just running to keep up with your sorry ass."

We finally calmed down and took stock of what had just happened, and we decided we weren't going down in that canyon again while the fire was down there—no matter who wanted us to.

Then Lisa reached down and pulled a rock out of her pack—the same rock—and said, "Okay, what sorry son-of-a-bitch put this in my pack?"

I tried to look innocent.

***

In 1983 Pope and Talbot, the largest mill in Oakridge, ran out of trees to cut. They gave the employees seventy-two hours' notice and pulled out, lock, stock, and barrel. Up until that time Oakridge had been a thriving small town of three thousand, with the mill being its largest employer. It was like Gary, Indiana, when the steel industry went to China, or Kentucky when the coal mines started shutting down. People who had been rolling in cash for decades with jobs they thought would go on forever were suddenly unemployed with no way to pay for food, shelter, or the big four-wheel-drive trucks they all drove. Other than unemployment, they had no means of supporting their families.

It was like a punch in the gut that knocked the wind out of the whole town. People were gathered in small groups, talking, trying to figure out what had just happened and how to go on. Little by little the town began dying, like a tree whose roots were rotted away and that first began dropping leaves, then branches—then finally toppling over. The bowling alley closed, no one had money for bowling. The Sportsman's Club—one of the most popular restaurants in town—closed, followed by other bars and cafes. The laundromat shut down, leaving people with no way to even wash their clothes.

Then the unemployment ran out.

The fact is, these people had put all their eggs in one basket, and they thought that basket would feed them forever. They gave their loyalty to the company and thought the loyalty would be returned. It wasn't, and finally they had to come to the realization that they had not been in charge of their own destinies; they had turned that over to someone else.

Townsfolk began looking for things to blame their predicament on: liberals, the damn environmentalists, the forest service...the list could go on. You can never run out of people to blame things on. Some moved to other towns, and some were able to get retrained in other professions, but just like with any other company town when the company goes down, some of them descended into various states of blame and self-pity.

Years later, now the land is beginning to recover from the scourge of massive clear-cuts. The deep ruts created from dragging logs through the once-verdant hillsides are healing over. The animals and plants will return and begin to establish the balance that has served them for centuries, and the land will slowly come back to its natural state.

Thirty years from now, the new trees will be merchantable timber, and we will again begin the harvest to supply the needed housing for our growing population. Gradually, we are beginning to realize that we can't just cut trees indiscriminately without regard for the fragile ecosystem. Maybe by that time, our forestry practices will have evolved enough to do responsible harvesting instead of cutting massive swaths through the forest. Maybe we will "select cut," taking only some of the trees and leaving some to grow. Someday we will manage our forests so that all our plants, animals, and kin can continue their lives with minimal impact, pretty much how the indigenous inhabitants had done for centuries.

As always, there's a core of forward-thinking folks who refuse to waste time blaming their predicament on someone else and have been exploring other options for Oakridge. It is a gateway to miles of mountain trails, lakes, and rivers, giving it an advantage over other towns in the same predicament. They are putting their plans to work, and the town is now moving successfully toward re-creating itself as a center for outdoor recreation, including mountain biking, fishing, and hiking.

Oakridge is a wonderful town in a beautiful location—and I hope they achieve long-term success. If you are ever in that part of the country you should pay them a visit. Do some fly-fishing on the crystal clear upper Willamette river, hike some of the backcountry trails and then eat at Middle Fork Bistro or Deep Woods Distillery. You'll love it and they will appreciate it!

Chapter 28

OUR CHILDREN, OUR STATEMENT

N ANCY AND I HAD been together for six years and after much contemplation and discussion, we finally came to the conclusion that if we were to bring children into this world, we'd raise them to be part of the solution, to join the army of good—to be Love Warriors—and that's what we've done. Our children have an extremely high system of ethics and will stand up for the underdog whenever possible. They take responsibility for their failings instead of looking for others to blame, and they strive to conduct their lives in an honorable manner. Our children are our statement that we are not willing to sit by without being participants in moving the world forward toward greater good.

We started while they were in the womb, playing many different types of music, from R&B and jazz to Bach and Brahms, and reading literature from different cultures—everything from Aesop's Fables to science journals. We continued reading to them when they were born, even before they could talk, exposing them to as much of the world as possible. When they began reading themselves, we would have a time each night where each one of us would take turns reading to the family. It didn't matter whether it was Archie comic books or *Goodnight Moon*—we were always reading.

We taught our children about the different ethnicities, philosophies, and religions of the world and gave them the choice of whether to participate in these arenas or not. We let them know we would support them no matter what path they chose. They both chose the religion of doing good for the world, which is fine with me. Our church is the great outdoors, and we attend services regularly.

When they were young, a typical Saturday morning was: "Okay, get your hiking shoes on—we're going on an adventure!" Sometimes we'd start out hiking, or sometimes we'd ride our bikes until we ran out of trail. Then we'd stash our bikes and crawl and slither through the brush until we were thoroughly lost—and then we'd find our way out again.

As I am writing this (2019), I am sitting beside Walton Lake in the Ochoco mountain range in eastern Oregon. Walton Lake is a beautiful spring-fed lake, surrounded by tall ponderosa pines with their distinctive red "puzzle piece" bark and green grassy meadows stretching for as far as I can see. I watch as a lone osprey folds its wings, expertly dips its talons into the water with barely a splash, and then struggles to gain altitude with a large rainbow trout gripped tightly in its claws. I hear coyotes sing and watch as a family of wild ducks feed on the rich plant and animal life beneath the surface.

My daughter Jazmin, the consummate chef, is frying bacon for breakfast. The aroma reaches my nostrils, awakens me from my meditations, and draws me back to the campsite. As anyone who spends time in the outdoors knows, food always tastes better when cooked outdoors.

As we sit down to eat, an older lady appears from somewhere in the campground. Platinum blond, dressed in denim stretch pants, sleeveless plaid shirt and cowboy boots, she gushes about how beautiful this place is and tells us about nearby wonders of nature that "you just have to see." She tells us about the humungous trout her husband pulled from the lake yesterday and what lure he used to catch it. As I sit and watch her gesture excitedly, I realize she is "high," but not on a chemical substance. I've seen it before: she is high on life, high on nature.

I suspect she may have different political and religious leanings than us—but it doesn't matter. That's one of the things about the outdoors. Most folks you meet on the trails, on the rivers and in the campgrounds have one thing in common: the love and appreciation of nature—everything else is secondary.

Later, we hike up Lookout Mountain, one of my favorite vistas in the world. We catch the distinctive musky scent of a herd of elk somewhere in the vicinity. We pass through groves of huge Douglas firs with tendrils of moss adorning their branches. We meander along the edge of a vast grassy plateau, broken here and there with rocky escarpments, until we finally reach our destination. We sit at the edge of a rocky cliff overlooking the Badger Creek Wilderness area with views of Mt. Hood, Mt. Adams, Mt. Rainier, Mt. St.

Helens, Mt. Adams, and Mt. Jefferson. The view is astounding, and we are mesmerized by the beauty of it all. The panorama is so picturesque I refuse to take pictures; photos fall flat and do no justice in describing the magnificence and grandeur of this spot. Better to drink it in, take a picture in my mind, and keep it in my soul as part of me forever.

Just when I think it can't get any better, my son Taj pulls a bottle of Jack Daniel's from his backpack—and the day is complete. I feel like I'm in a TV ad or something, and I almost expect a square-jawed logger dude clad in a plaid shirt and suspenders to walk out of the woods and say in a deep gravelly voice, "Life is better with Jack Daniel's."

We tend to seek the less-traveled trails. The few travelers we meet are always eager to tell us about other wonderful trails to walk and beautiful sights to see. We express our wonderment at the grandeur of it all, but like photos, words tend to fall flat in their descriptions, so we fall mute and allow it to become part of us, for us to be part of it.

This is our church; this is where we come to become invigorated, recharged; this is where we come to get inspiration and to connect with each other, with nature, and with God.

Chapter 29

BACK TO CINCY, 1986

WE HAD SETTLED INTO our little Oregon bubble. It was a place where you could safely walk the streets in pretty much any neighborhood, day or night, without fear of being mugged or being the victim of a random drive-by shooting. Although I acknowledged that this was not the reality many people in different parts of the country experienced, it was easy to get to the point where you began thinking things have gotten better everywhere.

In 1986 I went back to Cincy to visit my father during his prolonged battle with cancer. I took our three-year-old daughter with me so she could meet my dad and connect for the first time with her aunts, uncles, and cousins.

We arrived at my mom and dad's house in the evening, and, of course, it was even tinier than I remembered. The next morning after breakfast, I was excited to show Jazmin my old neighborhood. We started out walking the streets, headed for Montgomery Road, which was a popular hangout back in the day. As we walked, we constantly had to avoid broken glass strewn along our route. Several times I had to cross to the other side of the street to avoid having to step over people lying in our path who were either passed out on drugs, drunk, or dead (I didn't care to investigate which) or to avoid groups of dangerous-looking dudes blocking our path.

A tall, rangy-looking guy appeared out of an alley and said, "Hey, man, you got any money?" He looked like he had just woken from a long sleep: watery eyes, disheveled clothing, and the halting gait so many of the denizens of the drug world had, but I got the impression he always looked like that. He wasn't particularly aggressive—more pathetic than anything else. It was obvious some drug had inhabited his mind and body and occupied it much as the creature in the movie *Alien* occupied human bodies. He had no choice in the matter anymore; he was controlled by whatever substance he'd had the misfortune of letting into his body.

I replied, "no, not for you."

He looked disappointed and maybe thought about challenging my answer but somehow couldn't muster up the words or courage to do so—or maybe he forgot what he had asked. He moved out of the way, and we kept walking.

The neighborhood was full of overflowing garbage cans, mangy dogs running loose, and disheveled houses along our route. There was apparently no attempt at neighborhood improvement. Little by little my excitement turned to disappointment, apprehension, and then fear.

My old neighborhood, had in fact become a much dirtier and more dangerous place. I finally turned around, headed back to my mom's place, called my secretary, and asked her to make sure my life insurance was paid up. I didn't do any more exploring while I was there. When I left, I told my family, "I love you, but if you want to see me, you're going to have to come out West—I can't come back here again."

It wasn't that I thought I was better than that place or the people who lived there. I just remembered what a dangerous place it could be and how easy it was to cross paths with the wrong element and end up in the hospital or the morgue. I had been a different person when I had lived there; I hadn't had a family or employees and their families depending on me. I was determined to live to see my children grow up and to be able to play with my grandchildren. Getting messed up by some random drugged out dude on the streets of Cincinnati didn't fit with my plans.

I know that might come across as elitist or something, but that's just how I feel. I enjoy being able to take a nightly walk around my neighborhood without having to worry about being jumped or shot by some gangbanger trying to get street cred or a dollar. I have experienced a life where people smiled at you even if you were a stranger, a place where I didn't have to watch my back all the time. If I wanted to walk to the corner store at midnight, I could do that without a second thought. I would love to see a day when kids growing up in the South Side of Chicago or in Oakland neighborhoods could do the same. I wish everyone in every town had that same freedom.

I'm not naïve enough to think this could happen in one generation, or even two or three. But if we start now and touch one child who has no other outlet except the streets, that's a start. And if that one child grows up to be someone who makes a positive contribution to society and touches two other young people who are on the edge, just imagine what kind of multiplier effect that could have.

Chapter 30

IMPOSTER SYNDROME

THE GROUP OF GENTLEMEN filed into the room and seated themselves at my conference table. They all wore neatly pressed dark suits, neckties, and long-sleeve white shirts. They were part of a line of national and international companies wanting to do business with my company. I had built my business from a single-car garage to an international company with distributors in twelve different countries, we were the third largest in our industry. I had eighty-three employees and had built a large factory building to operate out of. I was the picture of a successful businessman.

We exchanged business cards and did introductions, but as we began our negotiations, I suddenly had a familiar and uncomfortable feeling and wondered, "When are they going to see through my façade and discover I have no business being here?"

I was a perfect example of "imposter syndrome," which is defined as:

Impostor syndrome (also known as impostor phenomenon, fraud syndrome or the impostor experience) is a concept describing individuals who are marked by an inability to internalize their accomplishments and have a persistent fear of being exposed as a "fraud." The term was coined in 1978 by clinical psychologists Pauline R. Clance and Suzanne A. Imes. Despite external evidence of their competence, those exhibiting the syndrome remain convinced that they are frauds and do not deserve the success they have achieved. Proof of success is dismissed as luck, timing, or as a result of deceiving others into thinking they are more intelligent and competent than they believe themselves to be.

—**Wikipedia**

Looking back, I realized I had in a large part done it to myself. It started when I was due to start high school. Back then they gave schoolchildren IQ tests and placed them accordingly. Thanks to my dad's lessons in deductive reasoning and my home environment, which stressed learning, I scored high on the test and was singled out to attend Walnut Hills High School.

Walnut Hills was what they called a college preparatory school and was where they sent all the high-achieving high-schoolers in Cincinnati, kids that showed promise—otherwise known as "eggheads." It was an elegant red-brick school surrounded by fourteen acres of rolling green hills. Approaching the entrance with its stately white columns, you felt as if you were entering the Greek halls of higher learning where you might run into Socrates, Plato, or Aristotle. Walnut Hills was ranked number one in Ohio and number eighteen in the country at that time and has been a jumping-off point for many talented and gifted young people.

There weren't many minorities in this school back then, except for my sister and a few brown faces scattered here and there. I'm sure my parents were exceptionally proud that I was accepted into Walnut Hills; it was the kind of school any parent would want their child to attend.

From the beginning, though, I felt uncomfortable at Walnut Hills: out of my element, away from my friends, and a Black face in a sea of White. I had the distinct feeling that I did not belong there. It wasn't that the other kids or the teachers were not welcoming. In fact, I don't remember any instances of racism directed toward me. Most of those kids were so busy trying to keep up with the workload, maybe they didn't have time to think about race. It was just that when I walked the halls and into every one of my classrooms and looked around, I was the only one. Maybe if I had been used to that from the beginning, I would have been okay with it, but I had been raised in a predominantly black neighborhood, went to a black church, and attended a very multiracial elementary and middle school, and that was my norm.

Adding to that, there was an accumulation of messages and images on television, in society, and in daily life indicating to young Black people that we were not as intelligent and able as our White counterparts. I know this is not true, but that message had been repeated in so many ways and for so long it had infiltrated my mind. To this day there are vestiges of that message still rolling around in my mind. I was afraid I did not measure up, that someone had made a mistake in reading the IQ test scores or mistook mine for some White kid's test.

Most of the images in the news, in movies, and on TV told us we were second-class citizens. The only roles for Black folks were as servants or as thugs, thieves and other less than honorable roles.

Common messages included, "Black people will never excel in math or science," and "Too bad he's Black; otherwise he might have made a good businessperson." Even in sports we got messages like, "Black people don't have the focus to do long-distance running," and "Black people can't possibly quarterback an NFL team; they don't have the intelligence to remember all of the plays and run a team." These ideas were constant and insidious. The Mormon church even proclaimed that Black folks did not have souls!

Most images of Black folks on the news were of Black people committing crimes. Watching the news, you'd think all we did was run around breaking into stores, robbing people, and raping White women. The Black inventors, those who ran businesses, and those who were in political offices didn't make the news. The vast majority who went to work every day, did an honest day's work, and went home to their families were not newsworthy—the Buffalo Soldiers and Tuskegee Airmen or even the 761st Tank Division were not in our history books. One of the most successful federal marshals in history, an escaped slave by the name of Bass Reeves—purported to be the basis for the story of the Lone Ranger—was not even mentioned.

It makes you wonder how many other Black heroes there are and have been that contributed to the success of this country but whose contributions have been buried.

I know all these messages are not true, but after seeing these negative images and hearing these racist words for so long, it was hard not to let them seep into your consciousness. And conversely, White people, who also saw such things repeatedly, had to begin to believe them, too.

The other part of it was that I was so connected to being part of the gang that to me, being sent to Walnut Hills was more of a punishment than a reward. The message I got was, if I achieved good grades and demonstrated intelligence, I would be separated from my friends.

So...I skipped school, read comic books, and did everything I could to flunk out. My teachers tried to intervene, and the principal called me in and tried to talk sense to me—I think he knew what I was doing. My parents and other relatives tried, but all to no avail. I really lived up to my "Rockhead" nickname.

Looking back now, I realize how frustrating it must have been for my parents and my teachers to see me squander such an opportunity. If I had it to do all over again, I would have learned the Latin they taught. I would have learned the higher math. I would have studied poetry, literature, and all the other things that make you a learned person—even if it wasn't cool.

Instead, I took a completely different path. After a year of this, I finally achieved my goal. I flunked out of Walnut Hills, much to the frustration of my teachers, my principal, and my parents.

When I got back to my neighborhood school, I decided I would never again do anything that made me stand out. I skipped school, continued with my pursuit of reading every comic book in print, and didn't participate in class discussions or activities. I did everything expected of a "D" student: just enough to get by and nothing more.

The problem is, after a while, I began to believe the internal dialogue I was streaming..

***

I continued this dialogue for most of my life until 1988, when I was working with music producer Pat Miller to create the music for the *Claymation Christmas Celebration* on the Atlantic Records label. Pat was the picture of positivity, the kind of person who didn't know the meaning of "I can't." To him those words just meant he hadn't found the way to do it yet. Pat was one of the most creative people I'd ever met, but looking at him, you'd think he was an NFL lineman or fullback. When we shook hands, it was as if my hand was engulfed in a five hundred-pound gorilla's hand, and it was questionable if I was going to get it back intact. His hugs were like being embraced by a grizzly bear—rib-crushing.

Between recording sessions, we would have conversations ranging anywhere from the best restaurants in town to ways to save the world. During one of our conversations, he stopped, and, probably in response to something I had said, reached over to grab a book from his shelf. He handed it to me and said, "Here, you need to read this."

I looked at the title of the book; it was *The Imposter Syndrome.* I looked at him for an explanation, and he said, "Just read it."

I took it home and read it, and he was right—I was the perfect example of the imposter syndrome.

I was convinced my professors gave me good grades as a favor, even though the tests I took were the same as everyone else's.

I was convinced any success I had achieved was purely by accident rather than something I had accomplished—even though I had worked my ass off for everything I had. And all the older established businesspeople who, for some reason, took an interest in me? Well, maybe they thought I was worth the time, but if they spent a lot of time with me, they'd surely come to the realization that I was not as smart as they thought I was. In other words, I thought that one day someone was going to blow the whistle and sound the alert, "He doesn't belong here!"

The thing is, intellectually, I knew I had a good mind, but I also realized there were kids in my neighborhood who were just as smart and smarter than me. The difference is that I came from a family that gave me a foundation on which to build, and when the time came, I was able to rise above the shackles I had allowed the world to place on me and me on myself.

As much as I tried to deny this, as much as I tried to sabotage myself, my parents' foundational lessons were imbedded in the innermost recesses of my mind, and after a considerable amount of work, they finally took. Many inner-city kids do not have that kind of foundation to nurture them.

Peer pressure persists to this day among many inner-city youth: don't talk White, don't get good grades, dress a certain way, walk a certain way; the pressure to conform in inner-city schools is intense. I wonder how many potential college graduates, attorneys, business executives, and politicians have been thwarted by the need to be part of inner-city coolness or to obtain street cred or whatever they call it now. I'm sure it is just as frustrating to parents, teachers, and others to watch intelligent young Black and Brown people succumb to peer pressure rather than step out and use their intelligence to excel.

I know I sound like a hypocrite or an "Uncle Tom" to some people, and fifty years ago I would have looked upon someone like myself as a sell-out.

As a kid growing up in the '50s and '60s there was a dearth of visible African American role models to look up to. The shining light for me was Sidney Poitier. Sidney was an actor who refused to be cast in the foot-shuffling, head-bowed Negro role so common in movies of that day. He dared to carry himself in a proud manner on stage; he spoke eloquently and was a hero in most of the roles he played. There were other role models we could have looked up to, but they weren't in the news or our books. They weren't called out in history, current events, or classes in school, so consequently we were not aware of the many accomplishments made by Black men and women. What we came away with from what we were taught in school was that White people performed all the actions, and Black folks were just acted upon.

It took years of self-improvement, affirmations, and hard work to get past these beliefs that had become intrinsic in my psyche. I feel that I've purged most of it, but vestiges of it are still there, and I'm constantly having to catch myself and autocorrect to stay on course.

Chapter 31

CUSTOM CRAFTWORKS, 1996

"H ow was your day today?"

It was an innocent enough question, and my wife Nancy had asked it countless times before. This time, though, when I opened my mouth to answer her, I instead found myself slumped to the floor with tears rolling down my face.

I was going to tell her payday was tomorrow, and I didn't know where I was going to get the money to pay my employees.

I was going to tell her the state tax collectors had shown up at the factory that week, ready to close us down for falling behind in our unemployment tax payment, and the only thing that had stopped them from locking our doors was that I had made arrangements with their home office to make payments to catch up on my back taxes.

I was going to tell her I was going to have to fire one of my employees, and that, even though he deserved it, firing someone was usually preceded with many conversations trying to bring the employee around and many sleepless nights trying to find a way to save their job. I always felt like I had failed them somehow. Adding to that, an employee I had been forced to let go had committed suicide days afterward, and even though the firing was justified and his friends and other employees insisted his suicide had nothing to do with him losing his job, it was hard not to feel responsible.

All these things and more were rolling around in my head and came to a boil when she asked that simple question. I'm normally in complete control of my emotions, but I found myself sitting on the kitchen floor with tears cascading down my face.

She looked at me and said, "Why don't you just give this business up and get a job working for someone else?"

I rose to my feet and said, "Work for someone else? No way—I'm going to make this work." And I did.

Little by little I began growing the business. I had three credit cards I regularly maxed out to buy supplies and materials. My friend Roger Galka had $5,000 he was going to invest in stocks but instead agreed to let me use the $5,000 as a line of credit. So, I would max out the cards to buy supplies, use Roger's $5,000 to pay down one of the cards, work on paying him back during the month, max the cards out again, borrow from Roger to pay the credit cards...around and around. There was no logical reason this would work, but it did.

I began hiring people to help make my tables and before long, I had sixteen employees—many of them ex-convicts, recovering alcoholics, and drug addicts. I spent much of my time being a counselor to these folks, trying to convince them that staying straight was worthwhile. Sometimes, I would have to run friends of my ex-con employees out of the parking lot because I didn't want them being a negative influence. My message to my folks was "If you want to break those old bad habits, you gotta separate from your old crowd."

One of my employees, Chad, had spent his entire adult life either in jail or behind the lines in Cambodia and Vietnam as an Army Special Forces Ranger. He was a big, scary-looking guy whose face showed the results of many fights; he had scars over his eyes and elsewhere on his face, and his nose was permanently pushed over to one side. His face said, "I'm nobody you want to fuck with."

We hired Chad because we suspected he was doing armed robberies around town, and we wanted to get him off the streets before he killed someone or ended up back in jail. Chad was someone who really wanted to change but didn't know how. I gave him books to read and tapes to listen to and spent hours talking to him about possibilities. I was making progress with him and feeling good about it, until one day he came to work early and said he needed his check. When asked why, he said, "Well, I have a feeling the cops might be coming to look for me, so I can't be here anymore."

That really sucked because I thought we had gotten over the hump. He was gone, never to return. Months later I got a letter from him apologizing for failing; he was back home—in jail.

The druggies were a scary lot because we had all kinds of whirling and cutting machines, and you really needed to be aware of what you were doing when operating them. Being stoned out of your mind was not a good thing in that environment. I tried to be there in the morning to look in people's eyes when they came to work and when they came back from lunch. If I suspected they were high, I'd pull them aside, take them over to the coffee shop, get some coffee in them, and give them the Talk. There were times when they would even nod off while I was talking with them.

After a couple of years of doing this, I realized I either had to commit to operating a profitable business or become a halfway house, but I couldn't do both. I started doing drug testing and lost half of my crew; some of them actually chose drugs over employment—but production—and attitudes went up tremendously.

I realized how much progress I had made in the industry when the major supplier of spa and massage equipment in the country called me and said, "Ron, the owner of the largest manufacturer of massage equipment in the country just visited my company and spent so much time bad-mouthing you and your company that I thought I'd better call you and find out why you were scaring him so much." In our conversation, we found that our outlooks on business and in life were remarkably similar and spent the next two hours mapping out a distribution agreement between our two companies. They became one of my largest distributors.

In six years, Custom Craftworks went from operating out of a single-car garage to a brand new 20,000 square foot factory building and being the third-largest company in the industry with numerous patents in the medical and massage industries. We had distributors all over the United States, South America, Australia, China, Japan, and Europe. By 1997 we were bringing around $6 million per year into the Oregon economy ($10 million in 2020 dollars) and providing above-average wages for scores of Oregon residents. I knew I was successful when, while walking though the airport in Zurich, Switzerland I saw three different products of ours being used or sold.

In the meantime, I had two other businesses going; one, BodyJaz, was a retail store and day spa. We were retailing massage essentials for professional massage therapists and home massage and high-end body lotions, candles, and sundries. We had a blending bar where a person could design their own perfume, lotion, or body butter with virtually any combination of scents and lotions. We also had sixteen massage therapists on staff and had a constant stream of people in and out of the store and massage center. It was a growing business, and I had plans to duplicate the concept and open franchises in other parts of the country

My other business, Valley Technology, was based around an invention I and a prominent anesthesiologist had developed and patented— the Epidural Positioning Device (EPD): a device used in labor and delivery that positions a patient while the anesthesiologist is performing an epidural—a procedure in which the doctor has to stick a long needle into the patient's spinal column and inject fluid into a precise area. Before our invention, they'd call a nurse, a relative, or sometimes even the janitor and have them try to hold the patient steady while performing the procedure. Needless to say, there were many horror stories surrounding this method. The EPD was introduced to hospitals in 2001 is presently used in hospitals around the world in labor and delivery and operating rooms.

In all, between the three businesses I had 103 employees working for me at any given time.

Chapter 32

A CHANGE IN THE MARKET, 2005

A S PART OF OUR marketing, we regularly attended the major spa and salon trade shows that took place in Las Vegas. These shows were some of the glitziest shows on earth. They have the latest in skin care products, and a was a showplace for upscale spa and massage equipment—which is why we were there. We were exhibiting at the 2005 International Spa and Aesthetics Show in Las Vegas, one of the largest shows for the industry. I always let my sales crew take care of the booth because they were so much better at it than I was. I generally spent my time cruising the show, looking at what was new and talking to other exhibitors.

During my first tour around the show I was amazed to see so many of our flagship Athena massage tables on display. I was feeling rather good that I had made such inroads into the spa industry. I stopped into one of these booths and struck up a conversation with the sales crew. It didn't take long for me to realize they had no idea who Custom Craftworks was, much less what the Athena was. I took a closer look at the table and realized it was not a Custom Craftworks table, but an incredibly good copy. I crawled under the table and saw the tell-tale "Made in China" sticker. I got up and did another tour of the show and realized a full 25 percent of the Athena tables on display were not Athenas, but Chinese copies. This was disappointing. I guess I should have been flattered that of all the tables on the market, they chose to copy mine—but I wasn't.

After returning home a couple of weeks later, there was a package delivered to the factory. Upon opening it I was amazed to see a copy of the Athena with a proposal from a Chinese middleman stating that we could buy this table from them for $65 delivered.

This price included materials, labor, shipping to a West Coast port and from there to our factory, payment to the manufacturer, and payment to the middleman.

My cost to manufacture this table was $220, and they were offering it to me for $65!

This was the beginning of the end of the domestic production of massage tables. One by one the companies in our industry folded, sold out to larger manufacturers, or began importing tables from China. I tried continuing with the "Made in America" theme, but even I had to hybridize our tables.

One example was my quest to find a two-cavity injection mold to use to manufacture a small plastic part for one of our products. I first tried sourcing it in the United States, and the lowest cost I could find after months of searching was $32,000—a price I could not justify for the part it was to produce. I then made a trip to China to source it and found I was able to have the same mold provided to me for $6,000, including shipping to my factory. I purchased the mold, brought it back to the USA, and had the parts manufactured here by a U.S. company. As much as I wanted to keep everything domestic, I just couldn't justify paying an extra $26,000 for the mold. This is the situation many U.S. companies have found themselves in, especially if they answer to a board of directors or stockholders who are bottom-line driven.

Eventually the Chinese manufacturers began marketing and selling in the U.S. through their own middlemen. I got frantic calls from other manufacturers in the industry asking, "What are you going to do?" We tried cutting costs and sharpening pencils, but our cost of labor and materials didn't allow us to get even close to the prices these imported tables were being sold for.

I traveled to China to investigate Chinese manufacturing and was amazed at what I saw there. Most glaringly was the disparity between the haves and the have-nots; it was appalling. I walked through neighborhoods where whole families lived on the sidewalk. Out of necessity they ate pretty much anything and everything. I've found that if I really want to experience a country and its people, there's no better way than to get out and walk the neighborhoods. So, after my meetings, I hit the streets and back alleys and walked the neighborhoods.

As I made my way through the alleys and backstreets of Shenzhen and Guangzhou I was greeted with open-eyed stares and looks of astonishment. I finally realized that most of these people had never actually seen a Black person in the flesh. I glanced back occasionally and realized I'd developed a following of a dozen or so people walking behind me, watching my every move. I didn't feel threatened; I thought I was just an object of curiosity. Finally, they grew tired of watching me and dropped off to go about their business.

I walked past open-air meat markets with displays of pig, poultry, and meats I didn't recognize and happened upon a man sitting in the background in the process of dismembering a freshly killed tiger. I pointed my camera toward him, and he immediately reacted to stop me. I quickly put my camera away and kept walking, but circled around and, on my second pass, surreptitiously snapped a photo. I assumed his fresh kill was highly illegal but would probably fetch a huge price on the illegal market.

Finally I emerged to find myself confronted by a huge stucco wall topped with rolls of barbed wire and sharpened wrought-iron stakes. I looked north and then south and realized the wall stretched as far as I could see in either direction. I chose a direction and walked until I finally came upon a massive metal gate. Peering through openings in the gate, I saw row after row of huge expensive houses—actually, not houses, mansions—with Rolls-Royces, Mercedes, and other expensive cars in front. Some even had chauffeurs standing by.

These must have been government officials and factory owners. I thought to myself, "So much for communism and all for the good of the people. I guess this must be human nature and the trickle-up theory, which seems to be prevalent pretty much wherever you go."

The manufacturing might in China is astounding; huge factories make everything from eyeglasses to jet engines. My friend took plans over for a product he had been making in the USA and asked what it would cost to be manufactured in China. He went to sleep that night, and when he woke the next morning, they had the prototype made and were ready to begin production for a fraction of what he had been paying in the U.S.

***

There is no point trying to grow grapes in Scotland, when they grow so plentifully in France. Countries should do what they are best at and trade their products. Restrictions on international trade inevitably make both sides poorer.

—**Adam Smith, *The Wealth of Nations***

Which means, theoretically, if China is the low-cost producer of massage tables, they should manufacture them for the rest of the world. Sounds good in theory, but nothing is that simple. Companies fail, industries fall, people lose jobs, and whole cities are affected.

The U.S. manufacturing base was moving overseas industry by industry. First textiles, an industry formerly centered on the Northeast and down through the Midwest, Appalachia, and southern states; then the steel industry, which devastated the Midwest, including Indiana, Illinois, and Pennsylvania; and then the secondary wood products industry went down, impacting the Pacific Northwest and Southeast. Coal, an industry centered in Appalachia and what workers in many states depended upon for their subsistence, was lost to automation. Towns died, and even large metropolitan areas were affected.

The result of these industries going down has been millions of already struggling blue-collar workers becoming totally disenfranchised. Some of these workers were able to be retrained for tech industries or other service industries, but many were stuck with subsisting on government assistance.

This brought to mind something I remembered hearing in one of Earl Nightingale's lectures. He was visiting a Midwest steel plant that had just shut down, where he encountered a group of bewildered workers standing in the parking lot.

He stopped and asked them, "Well, what are you going to do now?"

He got mostly angry comments about how the company, the country, and the industry had let them down.

Mr. Nightingale later remarked, "If these folks had taken a class one night a week for the thirty or so years they had been employed by the company, they could each have had a PhD by now."

This scenario was repeated time and time again across the country and in different industries. Even to this day, industries and companies are being affected by automation of processes that were once labor-intensive but are now done by robotics and machinery that can perform the process much faster, with more accuracy, and for far less. Or these jobs are outsourced to overseas manufacturers who don't have to deal with labor laws, unions, or paying living wages.

In October 2008, as most of us know, our economy took a dramatic hit. We had been heading into this recession for quite some time, but the Bush administration was not acknowledging it. Most of us were going about our business, working jobs or operating business as usual, when the bottom dropped out; we were caught unaware.

It was impossible to compete with Chinese imports while paying U.S. wages and having to deal with our regulations, taxes, and insurance. I saw the writing on the wall and made the decision to package Custom Craftworks and Valley Technology and sell to a company in the market for a business like ours—we came out fine.

I knew that the innovators in any industry are rarely the ones who profit the most when the product or service becomes mainstream enough to attract the big money. They rarely have the wherewithal or capital to compete on the level the big guns can.

Chapter 33

HAWAII VACATION, 2004

W HEN I LIVED IN Hawaii, one beach I never surfed was Makena Big Beach. Many of the local mothers wouldn't let their kids body surf at Big Beach because of the mean shore break that would sometimes pick you up, toss you around, and drive you headfirst into the sand. It also had an occasional riptide that was always changing the shape of the beach. There are probably more broken necks and dislocated shoulders at Makena Big Beach than any other beach in Hawaii, except for Sandy Beach on Oahu. This is where I found myself in 2004 while back on the island for vacation. We went to Big Beach just to lay on the beach and picnic; I had no intention of body surfing.

It was a typical Maui day: sunny, gentle trade winds blowing, *Kahoolawe* island in the distance. We were there for a picnic with friends and had a spread of beer, tuna sandwiches, Kim Chee, and Maui potato chips. I was standing on the beach talking with my son and his friend, when out of the corner of my eye I saw a wave approaching. I could have just backed up to avoid it, but I decided to dive under the wave instead. I got a running start and took a dive. What I thought was six feet of water was actually six inches, and I dove headfirst into the hard-packed sandy bottom.

It felt as if someone had thrown a concrete block and struck me in the head. I felt something pop, but being the hardheaded person I am, I thought nothing of it. I got up, walked over to Nancy, and asked for a beer because as we all know, beer cures everything.

Nancy looked at me with a concerned expression and asked, "Should I call an ambulance?"

I said, "No, I'm okay," but then the world started tilting and whirling in a way it shouldn't have. I thought better and said, "Yeah, maybe you should get them coming." We walked up to the road—something I later learned could have killed me—and stood there waiting.

While standing there on the road with my daughter Jazmin supporting me, my mind began to feel as if I was becoming disconnected from my body. The world began to take on a surreal look as if I was in a hazy two-dimensional dream; everything looked as if it was a film negative. Then the light of the world began to slowly fade away, with darkness taking its place. It was like an aperture on a camera that narrows and narrows until "fizzp"—the light is gone, and there's nothing. I didn't know whether I was passing out or dying. I told Jazmin, "Open the tailgate of the truck next to me because I think I'm going to fall in that direction."

She told me later that my eyes had clouded over and I had passed out. She thought I was dying, and she yelled for help. She also said there was a peculiar guy who was there by my side the whole time, not saying anything—just being there, a strong but comforting presence. Twenty years later, she still remembers him and wonders who he was. I've always said that the only reason I'm still alive is that I have a heavy-duty guardian angel. I don't know; maybe that was him?

Next thing I remember was the paramedics getting me onto a stretcher and loading me in the ambulance. When I got to the hospital they said, "Yes, indeed, you have broken your neck!"

I had broken my C-1 cervical vertebrae—you know, the area that controls your breathing, motion, all that stuff. When the nurse produced a pair of scissors, making motions toward cutting my swimming shorts off, I said, "Whoa, wait a minute! These are my brand-new trunks. I just bought these things!" Whereupon I lifted myself up to allow them to slip them off. Nancy loves to quote that as another example of my hardheaded nature.

While I lay in the ICU with sensors plugged in all over my body, one by one, nurses, doctors, and basically every medical professional on the floor poked their head in to look at me. I finally asked my doctor, "So, do I have a big booger in my nose or something? Why is everyone looking at me like that?"

He said, "They're just not used to anyone with your injury making it to the hospital alive." He called me "the miracle man."

I wasn't going to allow them to operate on me at Maui Memorial, which at the time was considered a one-way hospital. To be fair, some of the staff there were incredibly helpful including one nurse—I wish I could remember her name—who sat at my bedside and described to me the process of rehabilitating from a life-threatening injury, including the psychological effects of surviving a near-death event. I wish I had paid more attention.

Upon arriving back in home, I went to my doctor, who when he took one look at my X-ray and with a shocked look on his face said, "You need to be in a halo brace immediately!"

I argued with him until he showed me the X-ray. My C-1 vertebra was separated in two places by about nine millimeters, and there was a fragment of bone dangerously close to my spinal cord.

He said, "I'm not letting you leave the office without a halo brace. Are you okay with us installing it here in the office with no anesthesia?"

I said, "Of course, if that's what needs to happen."

He called the orthotic professional and had him come to the office to install the brace. What I didn't know is that they screw this contraption into your skull at four different points—the effect is like putting your head in a vice and cranking it down tight. It was like having a migraine magnified by twenty thousand percent. The orthotic specialist joked that the sheriff's department had said that if they could use this as a method to extract confessions from suspects, they would have no problem getting them to talk.

I spent months in the halo brace, trying to avoid the operation and hoping the cervical vertebrae would grow back together, but after five months—no success. I slept sitting up in my recliner every night and took sponge baths. The thing I missed most was being able to look up at the stars.

I convinced myself that I could make my C-1 vertebrae grow back together, which I had read was a possibility. I convinced my orthotic specialist to crank the halo brace up as tight as he could, stretching my neck and my cervical vertebrae, which in my mind would relieve some of the pressure and allow the healing to begin. That night, while sitting in my recliner, I heard a loud "POP," and it felt like the back of my head had caved in. Turns out, the screws in the back had been stressed to the point where they broke loose and created two deep furrows in my skull, which I still have today.

I finally submitted to having the operation, which involved taking bone from my hip, fusing it between my C-1 and C-2 cervical vertebra, inserting two massive titanium screws through the transverse process on both sides, inserting a metal plate, and wrapping it with cable to keep it stable. It was quite the process and a wonder of modern medicine. If I had suffered this injury fifty or even twenty years prior, I would have died.

This turned my head around more than I realized. All my life I had considered myself pretty much indestructible. I had jumped off tall buildings, fought fires, and felled massive trees, and I hadn't even had a cold or flu for going on thirteen years. This was the first time in my life I had been laid up for any period of time. My coat of armor had been pierced, and I had to face the fact that I was not invincible. It shook me to my core in a way that is hard to describe. I realized that my self-confidence was partly based on my assumptions that I could physically weather anything that came my way.

I began looking around and taking stock of what was important to me. I realized it wasn't money; I could make more money, and I had done without it for a period in my life. It wasn't how successful the business was. In fact, it didn't have anything to do with material things. It was family and friends—two things you cannot buy or replace.

Chapter 34

REBOOT VERSION II

2010

Don't die with your music still in you.

—Wayne Dyer

I was out salmon fishing off the Oregon Coast. It was one of those sparkling clear days with small, rolling waves, sunlight dancing off each roller as it crested and then succumbed to the transition from crest to trough. The seagulls were circling, waiting for scraps; the smell was a mixture of ocean spray, negative ions, and fish bait, a mixture impossible to imagine without being there.

We were trolling at a steady speed, hoping to hook into a school of salmon but having no luck. Nothing seemed to be interested in our bait. I noticed that occasionally the captain, a bewhiskered old sea dog who looked like he was born with a pipe in his mouth and the deck moving beneath his feet, would jump up the RPMs and put on a burst of speed, but just for a minute.

I asked him, "So, what's the purpose of revving up the speed like that?"

He said in his gruff whiskey voice, "Sometimes the fish get used to just following the bait, and it becomes mesmerizing to them. It takes something like the bait stopping or moving faster to bring them out of the spell."

For me, breaking my neck was like the captain speeding up the boat. It made me stop and take stock of what I was doing and whether I was happy doing it—whether I was doing it because it was just what I did, or whether it was something I really wanted to do.

The sale of the company had been a grueling experience that left me drained physically, mentally, and emotionally. My personality had been my corporations Custom Craftworks and Valley Technology for over twenty years, but now that was over, and I was swimming. Metaphorically speaking, it was time for another trip into the valley. My "valley" this time was a bit more comfortable than my time in Waikapu Valley, but I needed to accomplish the same goals.

I needed to do another reboot.

I took some time off, spending much of it by myself. I dusted off my *Tao Te Ching* and a few other books I had accumulated along the way and settled in for my second rebirth. It was exciting, venturing off into new but somewhat familiar territories again. I realized that this was an opportunity that few people get in their life, and I got to do it twice.

I sequestered myself during the day, reverting to my transcendental meditation practice. I began the process of breaking things down within myself and in my life, accepting the parts that worked and discarding the ones that didn't. I wanted to practice making lemonade.

Cooper, our ninety-seven-pound boxer, somehow sensed something important was happening because he stuck close to me—even closer than he normally did. Boxers have been called the philosophers of dog breeds because they seem to always be watching, observing, and understanding your moods. When he looked at me with his wise gaze and furrowed brow he seemed to be asking, "Hey, boss, anything I can do to help?"

I returned his gaze and said, "No, just being here with me is help enough." He couldn't recite pages from the *Tao Te Ching* or lay out the rebuilding process for me, but he was a wonderfully comforting presence.

I went through the many cards from friends around the world who had written to me during my recovery from my neck injury and sent psychic thank-you's to them all. I gave gratitude for my wonderful wife, who had become "Nurse Nancy" during my recovery and tended to my every need, and also for my mother-in-law, who had made several trips from Dearborn, Michigan to give support. I gave thanks for my tight-knit family who has always managed to stick together through thick and thin with overwhelming love for each other.

I realized I had never had time to fully process my neck injury. There's a kind of PTSD that comes with a near-death experience; you can see it in the eyes of people who have experienced it. It's something you can't really put into words, something that is a deep, integral part of us. There's a fuller appreciation of life, a realization of how precious our time is, and a tendency to savor every moment.

Coming close to death also shakes you to your core. The confidence I had built in myself over the years had dissipated. I wasn't conscious of it happening; I just noticed that I started approaching things with less surety. I even went through a period of anxiety, something I had never experienced before. I decided to let myself go with this downward spiral into the valley to see where it led and what I could learn from it.

I did not feel sorry for myself for having broken my neck; I realized it could have been so much worse. I could have been in a wheelchair for the remainder of my days, having to depend on others for many of my needs. I could have easily died there in the water and left my children to grow up without me. Every time I even thought about complaining about pain or a lack of mobility, someone would roll past in a wheelchair, or I would hear of someone dying from a similar injury, and it would remind me of how fortunate I was to be able to walk, talk, and breathe on my own—then I would stop and say a silent word of gratitude.

I began going through lists of things I'm grateful for, things I appreciate about life. I considered how temporary my time in this form is and how fortunate I am to be able to experience the wonderful things I have.

I appreciate the people in my life: what they mean to me, and what I mean to them.

Colors are brighter.

I savor every rainbow.

I wriggle my toes every morning because I can.

I love the rain because it touches my skin and reminds me that I'm alive.

I love the sun because it warms me.

I love the wind because it caresses me.

I love sitting in a coffee shop listening to Keith Jarrett in my earbuds.

I love getting caught in a sudden rain squall while walking on the beach.

I love getting a hug from my wife and kids when I leave in the morning and return at night.

I poke fun at my daughter for saying "love you" after every phone conversation, but I secretly love that she does.

I love that my son still calls me his best friend. I don't think a dad could ask for any more than that.

I appreciate the opportunity to make a difference in someone else's life.

And more than anything else, I appreciate life, love, and the opportunity to be on this beautiful Earth in this point in time—and I'm determined to make the best of it.

I've always made sure to spend quality time with my kids. If one of them calls me and says, "Hey, Dad, wanna meet me for coffee?" or "I'm going to hike Mt. Pisgah, wanna go?" My answer is always "Yes, when do you want to meet?" And my next call will be to cancel any other appointments I had scheduled.

I don't let little things bother me anymore. I tend to focus more on the macro and let minor things work themselves out, and if they don't, I deal with them and move on. People in my life who spout negative comments have tended to fade away; life is too short to listen to someone bitch and moan just for the sake of bitching and moaning. There are so many forward-thinking, positive people I can spend time with—after all, we do have a choice, don't we? If someone has a legitimate problem I can help them solve, and they are willing to do the work, I am fine with helping them, but I refuse to be dragged down into someone else's self-imposed rut.

Most of us—especially guys—tend to think of ourselves as invincible to some extent, and the thought of dying or becoming disabled just doesn't enter our minds until it almost happens. When it does, it changes how you look at the world and how you fit into it.

The world did fine before I came into it, and it will do fine when I'm gone, but MY world only exists while I'm in it, and I have to consider the possibility of my world not existing at some point. This is something I had never given any serious thought to before my accident. As I said earlier, I am totally fine with the concept of my death. And in an abstract way, I look forward to my next phase, but I thoroughly enjoy my life and value every moment I'm here in this body, in this form. I seem to have Wayne Dyer's words, "Don't die with your music still in you," running as a constant tape in my head.

Once you dig into your inner workings and let yourself go down into the valley, it can be tempting to stay there. There's a certain comfort in dwelling in the valley; it makes you want to wallow in the mud for a while. It's like enveloping yourself in a warm blanket, curling up in a corner, and sucking your thumb. It's a comforting place where you can retreat and lick your wounds and feel sorry for yourself. That's okay for a while, but it's important to not let yourself get too comfortable. I've got a saying I've always lived by and told others when I've noticed them getting too comfortable in their funk:

"Learn in the valley, but don't live in it."

It's a saying I've committed to print and hung on my wall, reminding me not to get too comfortable in the valley and linger there too long.

Without darkness, we would not appreciate light. I came out of the valley back into the light with my strength renewed, more grounded, and full of gratitude.

Chapter 35

NICARAGUA

M Y CHILDREN HAVE GROWN to be the "love warriors" that we were hoping for. Jazmin, from the time she was old enough to understand what injustice was, was in the fight for the underdog. While watching TV when she was five or six years old, an ad came on from one of the charity organizations asking for donations to help children in Africa. Jaz got a stricken look on her face, jumped up, ran in her room, and returned with her piggy bank full of her hard-earned coins. With tears in her eyes, she handed it to me and said, "We have to get this to them!"

Since then, Jazmin has spent her life reaching out to people, doing little and big things to help, and always being sincere in her offers.

She took up traveling around the world for a while—sometimes solo—to experience other cultures, something I wish every young person would do. During her travels she would stop in and volunteer with different organizations in whatever country she was in. By the time she was thirty-six she had spent time in thirty-seven countries. One of her stops was in Nicaragua, where she found herself in a small converted church building in the middle of an impoverished area of Granada. It was the home of Casa Xalteva, a nonprofit organization that accepted kids living in poverty and supported them through their schooling, offering daily meals, emotional support, and various extracurricular activities like classes in nutrition, dance, and English. Jazmin volunteered while she was there. When she came back to the U.S., she realized there was a need that wasn't being met at Casa Xalteva and wrote to the director of the organization with a proposal for a new position as a children's welfare coordinator. She made a commitment to return to Nicaragua and live there for a year to get the position started.

While she was there, my son Taj and I decided to visit her.

Flying toward Nicaragua, we saw miles of green verdant forests below stretching for as far as the eye could see, dotted with blue volcanic lagunes. But as we approached Managua, the capital city, the rich green gradually faded to a brown, arid-looking color, finally becoming a sick, parched dusty brown. All the trees had been cut to make way for cattle farming and other deforestation projects.

On the trip from the airport to Granada, where Casa Xalteva was located, we passed through miles of dirt-floored shanties with people hanging out on their stoops. We swerved to avoid a couple of men scuffling in the road, taking their frustrations out on each other. Nicaragua is a mixture of the extreme abject poverty of the local population and displays of wealth from the increasing number of expats getting priced out of Costa Rica and moving to the next Central American haven.

We finally arrived in Granada, where I met my smiling daughter. She had adopted this country, its people, and their way of life. A casual onlooker would be baffled as to why a young lady with an upper middle-class upbringing would trade her comfortable life in the U.S. for cramped, dusty, crime-ridden surroundings in the second-poorest country in the western hemisphere.

The answer came one night as we walked the streets of Granada. We were passing a group of restless young men I normally would be very wary of. They were hanging out in a dark alcove where we couldn't really see them, a boombox blasting Spanish rap music and the occasional tell-tale glow of a joint being passed around. Of course, Taj and I were on edge, being in a strange country, not knowing the language, and on a dark backstreet at night.

Then one of them yelled "Auntie Jazmin!" and ran out into the street to give her a big hug, followed by several other young men.

Later that night we visited the family of Juan Carlos, who was busy preparing a meal of tacos and popcorn for his family, two young ladies from Denmark, a young man from the UK, and a fearless young lady from the Netherlands. When we arrived, Juan Carlos, without missing a beat, increased the amount of food available to feed the added guests, almost like Jesus and the loaves of bread. We sat down to eat, and the fun and laughter continued. They poked fun at each other and at themselves; we enjoyed belly-hurting, tear-inducing laughter that continued into the night. I was not spared from the jousting, and I had learned just enough Spanish to strike back, bringing renewed bouts of laughter, which I suspected was directed as much at my poor attempts at speaking Spanish as at my bad jokes.

Jazmin has been robbed, hijacked, held hostage, and been witness to her friend's mugging—but her resolve and enthusiasm has never waned. She is a vibrant red rose in a field of brambles. The task of helping seems almost overwhelming when you see the almost indescribable poverty of the area. But I realize that Jazmin, her friend Marie, and the small troop of administrators and volunteers are doing something that many of us preach but few practice. It may seem like a drop in a vast ocean, but just as the ocean is made up of drops, they are two of the drops of humanity who strive to make a difference as they devote their attention wholeheartedly toward these kids.

The smiles and laughs made me realize that there was a sort of reciprocity happening at Casa Xalteva; the genuine laughter and playfulness these kids give is something money can't buy. They seem to appreciate life and the love that surrounds them. They have a twinkle in their eyes that I suspect would be hard to extinguish, and I hope that twinkle remains with them for their entire lives.

I appreciate that these volunteers give with no expectation of return. There is no alternative agenda, no religion or philosophy the recipients have to accept in order to receive; to me, that's the best part of their giving. It's pure, with no expectation of anything in return, just a desire to help these young people realize their own incredible potential.

***

On one of our hot summer days in Granada, Nicaragua, we were enjoying dinner at one of the outdoor cafes prevalent in that part of town. Patrons enjoyed the local wine and food, vendors sold sunglasses and fake jewelry, and local kids waited to see if there would be leftovers they could swoop in and gobble before the busboy got to them.

We couldn't help but overhear the conversation coming from the table next to us from two obviously affluent expats. We weren't eavesdropping—well, yes, we were. But in this situation, we couldn't help it. One of them was a tall, tan, good-looking surfer dude who obviously had both a backbone and brain extraction—a rare operation that sometimes coincides with too much time in the sun and way too many drugs. The woman had the good looks and an air about her that screamed, "Trust fund baby!" She had probably never worked a day in her life and was used to people bowing down and kissing her feet, which was pretty much what Surfer Dude was doing.

"But I just want to be your wingman!" he said to her in a puppy-dog voice.

"Well, I don't need a goddamn wingman!" she said, looking at him defiantly. "I can fend for myself! And what are you saying, anyway? I'm not capable of even walking home by myself?"

"No, I just want to be your protector. You are my goddess, and I'm your wingman."

It had started with a simple "Can I walk you home tonight?" It was a seemingly gallant request that in most situations would have been met with "Well, that's nice of you" or something of that nature. But she was having none of it.

In some part of his mind he realized he had gotten off on the wrong foot—but he didn't know how he got there or how to get out of it. He was trying to dig himself out of a situation that had gotten turned around into something else—you know, like when your girlfriend asks you if this dress makes her butt look big, and you tell her the truth.

"Why do you want to walk me home? You don't think I'm capable of walking home alone? Is that how you think of me: a defenseless little damsel in distress?"

I looked over at him and saw a look of bewilderment on the young man's face, bordering on panic. I almost felt sorry for him.

He didn't realize there was no way out, so he started in on trying to explain. "No, I respect your goddess-ness; I hold you high on a pedestal."

Who the hell talks like that? Had this guy been reading too many romance novels or something?

"I just want to be your wingman!" he finished.

There it was again!

By then we were having a hard time maintaining our concentration and I was refusing to look at Jazmin. She has a way of looking at me with wide eyes and a slight smirk on her lips—not a smile, not a laugh, just a little smirk—and she and I both knew that if I looked in her direction that would be the end of it. I would burst out laughing, and this was not the place for it. So, I tried to keep our conversation going, looking only in Taj's direction.

This is the Tinsley curse. My sister once broke out laughing at her friend's funeral because someone who had no business singing insisted on singing. She laughed so hard that people in the front pews thought she was crying. We will laugh in the sad part of a movie. We will laugh when someone trips up the stairs, and when someone needs a little pity, well...expect a laugh instead.

By then the conversation next to us had gone south, and the tall, tan surfer with the brain extraction was pleading:

"I respect everything about you. I worship the ground that you walk on; all I want to do is to be your wingman."

There it was again!

It was at that point I glanced in Jazmin's direction, and there it was: the smirk. The same smirk that had gotten me at the county fair when the lady with the generous backside was bending over scooping ice cream and straightened up to reveal that her name tag said, "Bernice Butt."

I felt the laugh begin to rise up inside of me like a giant bubble that wanted nothing more than to escape and become a gut-busting laugh. I didn't want to look in the couple's direction because I feared he might be on his knees licking her toes—or worse. I started laughing and rushed for the entrance and down the alley. I'm sure people thought I was bent over heaving because I could see them crossing the street to avoid me. That only made me laugh harder. Out of the corner of my eye I could see that Taj was trying to hold his laugh in.

And Jazmin just sat there with her little smirk.

Chapter 36

THEM THAT'S GOT

Them that's got shall get
Them that's not shall lose
So the Bible said and it still is news
Mama may have, Papa may have
But God bless the child that's got his own
—God Bless the Child, Composed and Sung by
Billie Holiday

I'VE ALWAYS BEEN SENSITIVE to the inequality created by our society's tendency to concentrate only on the young people with means to easily move forward in life due to their ascribed status, while ignoring the vast potential of young folks who are not fortunate enough to be born into families with means or ancestries that they can just tap into for a path to success.

The fact is, if one of us is in want, all of us are in want. There's a segment of our population that believes everyone should be able to pull themselves up by their bootstraps. But consider the young lady in Appalachia born into a family that has had to scrape by every day to make ends meet. She may be so consumed with scratching out a living that she has no time to think about pulling herself up by her bootstraps; she may not even have shoes to wear. Or the young man in inner-city Chicago who must use all his wits to avoid street violence, or the single mom who is one paycheck from being homeless. Then there are the people who through no fault of their own just don't have the mental, physical, or psychological ability to conduct themselves in everyday life.

Earlier in my business career I was having a conversation with a young Black man who had grown up on the west side of Newark, New Jersey, and had just arrived in Oregon. When it came out that I had businesses employing over a hundred people, he looked at me and said, "We can't do something like that!" At first I thought he was joking, but then I realized he really didn't think we could. His world had been one of clawing and scraping to make ends meet. His mother was a housekeeper with four children to support, and his father had been killed, shot down on the streets. He pulled up his shirt to show two healed bullet wounds in his own torso.

That was his reality. If he had acknowledged that anything other than that reality was possible, he and his family would have had to acknowledge how destitute their lives had been. It was easier to develop a separate reality that said, "This is the real world that we are living in here in West Side Newark—that other shit ain't real."

So many people are so stuck on the bottom rungs of Maslow's hierarchy of needs that they don't have the time, energy, or wherewithal to conceive of attending college or any of the things accepted as a given for the Haves, so they are destined to stay where they are. The economic barriers are significant, but the psychological hurdles are even more challenging to overcome and harder still to explain to someone who has never experienced them.

Unless they are somehow exposed to a mentor along the way, or if they are given a boost high enough to see over the edge, there's a good chance they're going to follow the route most of their peers and family members take, which could lead to life on the streets, getting into gangs, drugs, and—for far too many—jail. The mentor could come in the form of a teacher who shows interest and gives encouragement, a relative who takes time to listen and not judge, a role model, a peer—even a good cop who is doing his or her job correctly. Getting a nudge or word of encouragement at the right time could instead lead these people to a life of healthy contribution to society instead of being a problem.

There's such a vast amount of potential tied up in our youth. If they could be just given the means, the dream, or the realization of the possibilities awaiting them, we could find out what great things they could accomplish. But instead, we concentrate on the chosen few who are lucky enough to have had a silver spoon carefully inserted in their rectum at birth.

We, as a country, are a large organism that needs all our parts functioning to continue the upward trend we've been experiencing. It's been shown that we can't just leave things in the hands of the politicians, whether they be on the left or the right. We need to hold them accountable and ensure they are working for our interests, not just their own. Many of them are there for the right reasons, but so many of them succumb to the incredible amount of power that comes with holding a political office.

They forget they are there to serve ALL the people, not just the ones who voted for them. That means:

ALL the people—not just members of their own party;

ALL the people—regardless of race, religion, or sexual orientation;

NOT JUST SOME OF THE PEOPLE—ALL THE PEOPLE.

I see citizens flying the flag and spouting off about making America great again, but at the same time voting down school measures that would improve our school system and provide access to quality education for all. Keeping America great means starting now to restructure our educational system so that it benefits all children, regardless of race, geographic location, or their parents' financial status. It means restructuring our police and judicial system so that many of our Black youth don't unnecessarily end up in jail. We need to pour money, planning, and energy into social programs that serve to break the cycle that so many of these kids are trapped in. The system needs to work for all of us. Children of today are the future of our country. Think of all the progress we could make by just ensuring all children had quality education: how much less crime there would be, how these kids could grow up to be contributors to our society and economy instead of potential problems. It seems so basic, but we have yet to grasp this simple concept.

My hope is that someday our politicians will awaken to the vast promise and potential of these underprivileged young people and take steps to ensure they are not forgotten but are instead given the opportunity to realize their full potential for their own good and for the benefit of all.

It's easier to build strong children than to repair broken men.
—Frederick Douglass

Don't judge each day by the harvest you reap but by the seeds that you plant.
—Robert Louis Stevenson

Chapter 37

WHY ARE YOU BLACK GUYS SO ANGRY?

T HE OREGON COAST IS one of the most beautiful coastlines on the planet: wide white sand beaches stretching for miles, rugged cliffs, and expansive views. Visiting the Oregon coast gives one a sense of rejuvenation that's hard to explain. Some say it's the negative ions from the waves crashing against the shore, some say it's the sense of oneness with the earth that you can experience from looking out at the curvature of the earth. I don't question it; I just know that I will always live close to the ocean for my mental and spiritual well-being.

I've spent many days on the Oregon coast, hours of fishing, crabbing, and enjoying the fragrant mixture of seaweed, fish, and salt air.

I've explored the beaches, jetties, and bays from Astoria to Brook-ings—so I know a bit about the coast.

On this particular day I was in Newport, a mid-sized port town that is a take-off point for commercial fishing and crabbing fleets as well as charter fishing cruises trolling for salmon, tuna and the ugly but delicious ling cod. It was one of those beautiful September coast days with dazzling sun, blue-green ocean and just a light wind. I was there with a good friend for a day of fishing on the South Jetty hoping to land something to bring home for dinner. Notice I said "fishing" and not "catching"— there is a big difference. I spend much more time fishing than I do catching, and that's all right with me. Fishing for me is just another excuse to get on the water and away from any hubbub or stress of life. I measure my quality of life by the number of times I go fishing in a year.

After "fishing" for most of the day, we finally gave up and walked back to the car, skunked again! We had put our gear away and were standing at the car talking when an elderly couple approached us. He was a white-haired gentleman wearing a neat white sports coat, sharply creased slacks, and polished leather shoes. He wore a white straw hat perched on a head of white hair and sported a perfectly shaped goatee; reminded me of Colonel Sanders. He walked with a cane but carried himself in a dignified manner as if he was on his way to address the king or some other dignitary.

She was the picture of the Southern Belle with coiffed hair, small handbag, and white gloves. The scent of her perfume preceded her even with the coastal wind. A sweet rose-based scent that many older women favor but seems to have been passed over by younger generations in favor of more earthy scents. They both looked to be in their 80's but fit for their age. Neither of them was dressed for the beach, they looked about as out of place as a logger at a women's auxiliary meeting.

As they approached, he asked, "Excuse me, but is there a nice walking beach somewhere in the vicinity?"

I was familiar with that part of the coast, so I turned to him and said, "Actually one of the best walking beaches on the coast is just South of the jetty, it's a nice white sand beach that goes on for a couple of miles."

The man looked at my friend (who was white) and said in his southern drawl, "Thank you so much; now can you kindly tell us how to get to that beach?"

I thought the wind had snatched my words away and placed them in my friends' mouth, so I answered again; "If you just head for that notch in the sand dune over there you'll see a path leading to the beach – just be sure and stay back from the water and watch out for sneaker waves."

He looked at my friend again and said, "Thank you so much for helping us."

I had an overwhelming urge to jump in the car and look in the mirror, I thought surely, I must have suddenly become invisible or had become so ugly that he just couldn't bear looking at me—then I realized it was a "Soft Hit." The Colonel probably didn't even realize that he had delivered it, he was no doubt so used to not acknowledging black folks that it was just natural to him. My friend didn't catch it because he wasn't attuned to these slights, he had probably never had one directed at him.

Much as children at one time were to be seen and not heard, minorities for centuries in the U.S were not taken seriously unless they were in the company of a validating white person. They could then pretend that the words had come from the white person with whom they could safely interact without acknowledging the intellect of the black person in front of them. This saved them the trouble of confronting the fallacies that have been so embedded in their culture. It's easier for them to just "go with the flow," that way they didn't have to question whether black folks have an intellect or not, they just went under the assumption that we didn't, and we still had the proverbial tail growing out of our backside. It also prevents them from having to confront the possibility that this Black person in front of them might as smart or even (gasp) be smarter than them.

Most black folks have had the unpleasant experience of being invisible at some point in their lives. It's like some people can't accept the fact that we can think, talk, or say anything of any importance. Imagine a person with that attitude and their reaction to a Black president; it's Sammy T all over again, except I'm not there to talk them through it. They just can't bring themselves to accept it because it would violate everything they have believed in their entire lives and would violate every tenet of their upbringing. In fact, many people who practice this form of racism, now called microaggression, are not even aware they are doing it and would probably become defensive if you called them on it.

Microaggression—a comment or action that subtly and often unconsciously or unintentionally expresses a prejudiced attitude toward a member of a marginalized group (such as a racial minority)

—Merriam-Webster Dictionary

We may be tempted to give up on people like this, but my feeling is that many of them can in fact change. Again, we must decide whether it's worth our time to take on their re-education. It takes time, patience, and an understanding of how they got to where they are to begin to facilitate the change, but first, we have to determine whether it's worth our time and energy.

From working in many different parts of the country, in some places where many Black folks fear to tread, I've had the opportunity to be an "ambassador" for our race. Sometimes I'm met with standoffishness and even outright animosity when I first come on the scene. What I've learned though is that if I return the hard looks and harsh words, the situation just goes from bad to worse and it only serves to validate their fears.

If, however, I refuse to let it get under my skin and instead acknowledge their feelings—which are usually fear-based—I can slowly work to get to the underlying cause of their beliefs and begin to correct the misconceptions they've been carrying about minorities. Most times, the first step is to find some way to assure them that I'm not a threat to them, their families, and their communities and once I accomplish this, things seem to lighten up a bit and we can begin with their re-education.

My God—we've got a lot of work to do!

***

Hard Hits

"To be a Black man in this country and to be relatively conscious is to be in a rage almost all the time."
—James Baldwin

The most envied member of any band is the flute player. While the drummer is making multiple trips to the van hauling her fifteen pieces of equipment into the club, assembling high-hats, cymbals, a snare, tom drums, various pedals, and other items; the bass player is risking back injuries heaving his massive amplifiers in place and maneuvering a huge standup bass out of his little Honda Civic and through a door not meant to accommodate something so large; and the keyboard player is setting up her keyboard, stand, and amplifiers—the flute player prances in, opens his tiny fourteen-inch black flute case, removes his ten-ounce flute, assembles the parts, and is ready to play.

As a vocalist I sometimes had to provide the P.A. system for a gig, which consisted of two large speakers, two monitor speakers, speaker stands, mike stands, microphones, and what seems like miles of cable.

One hot August day in 1984, I was preparing to load my van for a gig at one of our many jazz venues that we were lucky to have at the time. This time I had help, though. My friend Bernard had been hanging at the house with me all day and decided to help me load and unload. Of course, I was thankful for the help.

We got the van loaded and headed for the gig. I always looked forward to playing at the Electric Station; we usually had a packed house, and the room had wonderful acoustics so I was in a really good mood. On our way through downtown I was surprised to see in my rearview mirror a police cruiser with his lights flashing, motioning for me to pull over. I knew I wasn't speeding, and I was pretty sure all my lights were operational because I had just checked. The officer motioned for me to pull into the Fifth Street Public Market parking lot, so of course I complied.

When the officer approached, I asked, "What's the problem, Officer?"

He replied in a cold, stern voice, "Step out of the car, please, and show your ID."

Bernard and I stepped out of the van, and the officer promptly put us up against the car and told us to stay there while he checked on our IDs and my car registration. He went back to his patrol car and talked on his radio for what seemed to me like a long time.

A little concerned that he had spent so much time on his radio, I asked again when he returned, "So, what's the problem, Officer? Why did you stop us?"

He replied, "You match the description of two suspects in a robbery nearby."

I asked, "What was the description?" even though I already knew what it would be.

He replied, "Two Black males."

I thought to myself, *I wonder if he stops every White male passing through downtown whenever a White guy robs a store?* I knew the answer: of course not. But I didn't challenge it; I didn't want to get choked out.

I was beginning to get pissed, though. I thought we were past this by now, but I waited—up against the car— in full view of everyone in the Fifth Street Public Market and everyone driving past. Another police cruiser pulled up with an older White lady in the back seat. She looked nervous as she peered out the window at us; she looked down, looked at us again, and turned away as the officer asked her something. I'm assuming he was asking, "Are these the guys?"

She looked again. She seemed uncertain, unable to make up her mind—I held my breath because I knew my future was in her hands.

She finally turned to the officer and shook her head. Whereupon the first officer looked at us, slightly disappointed. He gave our IDs back and said, "Okay, you can go now."

He did not say, "I'm sorry for taking your time, sir."

Nor did he say, "My apologies for putting you on public display in one of the busiest intersections in town while people drove by and gawked at you as you were up against a car."

Not even, "I promise not to embarrass you again."

None of that. Just "You can go now." Like I was supposed to thank him for not arresting me.

I would have loved to tell him what I thought of the situation, but I was so pissed that I was afraid to open my mouth.

Sandra Bland, a young Black woman in Waller County, Texas, dared to question an officer when she was pulled over. She ended up in jail where, being so distraught by her mistreatment by the arresting officer, she hanged herself.

Recently in Georgia, Ahmaud Arbery, a young Black man out for a jog, was run down, tackled, and killed by White vigilante, his son and a former investigator for the district attorney's office because he had the misfortune of jogging through a neighborhood that had been having a series of robberies. They didn't even have a description of the robbery suspect but must have assumed that a Black man running in the neighborhood must be their guy—so they killed him.

A few days later an officer knelt on George Floyd's neck until he died while George pleaded with him that he couldn't breathe. Stephon Clark, a young Black man in Sacramento, California, was shot and killed by police while in his grandmother's backyard, just using his cell phone. I could fill this book with names of the innocent Black people who have been killed by law enforcement with no recourse, no convictions—sometimes not even a serious investigation.

Lots of White people think this is a new phenomenon, but Black people know it's not. This same scenario has been playing out for centuries in this country. The only difference now is cell phones and body cameras and the ability to catch these situations on tape; and when the police officers lie—as they sometimes do—we have video evidence that they are being untruthful.

In most states hunting season for deer, elk, and other species happens only during certain parts of the year. If you are caught killing a deer out of season, you will almost certainly be convicted of poaching, and there will be repercussions. It seems, though, that hunting season for Black males is every day, all year long. The conviction rate for cops who kill innocent Black males is near zero—even when they are caught on tape!

When I had that encounter with a policeman, I had a wife and two children at home who depended on me to make the right choice and come home to them. I had to reflect on an incident from back in Ohio, when I had been around ten or eleven. Two White guys called my dad a nigger and pushed him around while we were in Norwood taking my dog to the vet. I was angry with him at the time for not speaking up and defending himself. I now realize he must have felt the same thing that I felt with the policeman—he had had a wife and five children who needed him to come home alive every day, and if he didn't, we would have been out on the streets. He kept his mouth shut because he knew what the outcome could have been. Sorry for judging you, Dad; I didn't know then what I know now.

Every incident a Black man has with a White person, if escalated, can lead to the arrival of police and result in arrest, injury, or death to the Black man. This is what is always in the back of our minds. That is why we are sometimes hesitant to call the police, and that's why we don't always consider them our protectors, but rather our adversaries.

So, I accepted the officer's lack of apology and slowly drove out of the parking lot past the group of onlookers who had stopped to watch the two Black criminals up against the car. I drove to the nightclub, pulled into the parking lot, unloaded my gear, got up on stage, put a smile on my face, and the show went on.

The smile was only skin-deep, though. What had started out as a beautiful day ended up bringing back memories of all the times I'd been threatened by police, knowing the brutality they are capable of. I've seen it enough to know there are some officers in it for the wrong reasons—on power trips, feeling like they are above the law. In effect, they *are* above it, given the immunity they enjoy. It creates an extremely stressful situation for a Black man. This is the cause for the "Black rage" that we occasionally see, when the pressure cooker that resides within most Black men finally erupts.

Then people say, "Why are Black guys so angry?"

To be fair, our police department has made some positive changes since then. Eugene has developed a system that includes social workers employed by Cahoots who have become the first responders for domestic disturbances and other nonviolent situations. This frees the police from having to deal with these events and lessens the stress load for them.

Cahoots is a mobile crisis intervention program that works through White Bird Clinic, providing free, confidential services to the public. Each Cahoots team consists of a mental health worker and an emergency medical technician. When you call the police in Eugene for any situation that does not involve violence or life-threatening medical situations, you will be routed to Cahoots; around twenty percent of 911 calls go to Cahoots. Statistics show that the Cahoots crew is ninety-nine percent successful in diffusing situations, whereas the police often just exacerbate them. This also results in a $15 million cost savings to the city.

To quote a Cahoots team member:

The tools that I carry are my training. I carry my de-escalation training, my crisis training and a knowledge of our local resources and how to appropriately apply them. I don't have any weapons, and I've never found that I needed them.

I really want to support our police departments. I feel they are necessary to keep us safe. I know all police are not jerks. There are so many of them who wear the uniform, badge, and gun for the right reasons, but—and this is a gigantic BUT—they all need to be held accountable just like everyone else. Just because you wear a badge does not mean you're above the law. The hiring practices of police departments need to be reconstructed to weed out the bad, and when a bad seed gets through and reveals his/her true self, they should be purged from the force. Also, if they commit a crime they should do the time just like anyone else.

Any hint of racism, whether overt or subtle, should be immediately addressed—there is too much at stake not to do so. Other officers who are there for the right reasons should do what they can to facilitate the purging of the bad apples in departments and stop the beatings and murders other cops commit. The brotherhood and the informal code that often prevents them from interfering must be disbanded for the good of all—including the good cops. We are paying them to protect us, not each other.

In addition, the "qualified immunity" that police unions have negotiated is like a license to kill and should be struck from every lawbook in the country. There is no need for it if police officers are doing their job correctly and protecting the public. I also realize that the attitudes many men and women in uniform carry are a reflection of the image of Black people that is pervasive in our society. It's evident in the lack of convictions in the few cases where an officer is brought to court, even with overwhelming evidence that they killed for the wrong reasons. When you get a chance, look up qualified immunity and how police departments have used this to avoid prosecution—I guarantee you will be flabbergasted!

As I sit and write today, on May 30, 2020, there are protests taking place across the country and even in sleepy little Oregon town. There are not just Black folks out in the street, but also Whites, Hispanics, and people of all races and walks of life. In fact, the majority of the protesters are White folks who see the injustices being done to minorities and are fed up with it. The protests have even spread to other countries—it should be an embarrassment to every United States citizen that citizens of other countries have to protest for the rights of Black Americans. But it is not, which is worrisome.

When I go out into rural America, the feel is much different. There is intense resistance to the Black Lives Matter movement. I wonder what scares them so much. Are they so insecure that the thought of us having rights, education, and employment opportunities equal to what they have always enjoyed threatens them? Or do they just not understand?

I think part of it is that they don't understand that when we say "Black Lives Matter," what we mean is "Black Lives Matter, Too." Of course, all lives matter; we just want to be sure to be included. We've been left out of the game in the past, and we want to ensure that we will be included in the future.

We don't want revenge. We don't want bad things for you. All we want is for opportunities to be evenly balanced. We want to be able to obtain good education for our children—the same as you want for yours. We want to be able to call the cops and have them come to protect us. We just want the opportunities that you take so much for granted that you don't even realize you have them.

***

When Barack Obama was elected president, many people felt we had arrived and that racism was dead in this country. We became complacent and quit paying attention. Racism wasn't dead though; it was still there, just waiting for the opportunity to raise its ugly head.

The White American male had enjoyed free reign over people of color, women, animals, and (if you asked them) every living thing for so long that the prospect of having a person of color in a position of power virtually sent them into a tizzy. For eight years politicians on the right side of the aisle systematically blocked everything Obama tried to do for our country, many times to the detriment of the country and their own constituency. It was like someone after losing an argument, out of spite going home and burning their own house down—then shitting on their front lawn.

When "45" gained the White House, he set about disassembling every bill that had Obama's stamp on it, also to the detriment of the country. This included attempting to dismantle the Affordable Care Act, simply because it had Obama's name on it, knowing that one of the effects of doing so would be to deny Americans, both White and Black, the healthcare we all need. We were all distraught that such a misogynistic, outright racist was going to be in the White House for four years. Many felt he was responsible for the racist behavior that has been brought forth. I would contend that it was always there, and we should thank him for making the other racists show their faces so that we now know who they are. It's much easier to address a visible threat than one that hides in the shadows.

Now that they are out in the open, if only we could have a big holographic "R" placed on each of their foreheads so when we are trying to reason with them and wondering why we are not making progress, or when we are experiencing one of those moments of covert racism and we're uncertain of where it's coming from, we could turn on our holographic reader, see the big "R" for racist on the forehead and go, "Oh...okay. Now I understand!"

When your significant other walks in the room and says, "We need to talk," you know that your best option is to stop whatever you are doing and pay attention. Well, I'm saying, "America, we need to talk!" Not only that, but also, "We need to listen." We need to have a forum where White folks and Black folks can talk and listen to each other without judgment, without fear of recrimination. We need to talk *with* each other instead of *at* each other. There's so much to be gained by getting to know people with different backgrounds and outlooks than ours; most times the monster under the bed is not nearly as threatening to you as you imagine it to be. If we take the time to understand each other's wants, needs, and fears, I think we will find that we have more in common than not. As for the things we don't agree on, maybe we'll learn to accept that about each other also.

Many of the people who are so adamantly against Black progress have been primed to believe that African Americans are the threat, that we are the cause for every bad thing that has happened to them. Meanwhile, the oligarchs have also kept the knee on their necks by pointing the blame to us for their woes instead of where the real blame lies. That is the system that has managed to keep all of us separated and at each other's throats while they go about their manipulative business of controlling us all.

The demonstrations and changes taking place today are another major step in our country's evolution. If you watch FOX news or Newsmax, the demonstrators are portrayed as anti-Americans intent on bringing down the government—a threat to our very existence. If you go out among the demonstrators, you'll find something quite different. You'll find that most of them are everyday people trying to institute change in America, young people of all races who are refusing to buy into the old paradigm, mothers wanting to make things better for their children and people just wanting to be heard.

Unfortunately, there are always a few people who resort to violence, and it sucks that the media has chosen to focus on them—but those folks are a small minority and are not representative of the protesters who are out in the streets for the right reasons. In fact, most of them want to bring an end to institutional racism in the police department, in our school system—in our country.

By the very fact that these folks are in the streets week after week, under threat of being tear-gassed, beaten, or arrested, instead of being at home watching television or playing cards, should make us realize the seriousness of what they are protesting. Pay attention—there must be something to it.

Systemic racism is like a five hundred-pound weight that Black folks don every morning when they step out into the world. It's like a high school bully waiting outside your door. Not only that, he's at your school, at your workplace, in the police cruiser driving by—hell, for a while, he was even in the White House. It's like a herpes sore that keeps coming back, or a weed that re-seeds and won't go away. Racism generates a pit in the bottom of your stomach and is, no doubt, one of the reasons suicide rates among Black youths between the ages of five and eleven are the highest in the country when compared to that of other ethnicities in the U.S.

If we let it, racism can keep us from moving forward; and I'm not just talking about Black folks. There's an opportunity cost White people pay when they devote so much of their energy to keeping Black people down. While they are doing that, they are not doing the positive things they should be doing to move themselves, their families, and their country forward.

Makes you wonder: What's so important about this quest to oppress Black folks that they would take so much time out of their lives to pay that opportunity cost? I wonder if they've ever sat down and examined where this need comes from. Is it something they came up with themselves—or are they pawns to someone else's master plan? (To get an idea of the master plan, read Nancy MacLean's book—Democracy in Chains.)

I don't think they know, and if you asked them, you would prob-ably find their words are remarkably similar to each other's. And if you looked deeper, you would hear the words of people like Rush Limbaugh, Donald Trump, Adolf Hitler, or master planners like John Calhoun and James Buchanan, who have dictated to them what to feel, what to say. These people have given them catchphras-es that are not original, just rehashes of idioms told to them to make them believe that other races are below them—all so that they wouldn't look up at the puppet masters pulling their strings. If they were able to come to a point where they had original thoughts, they would realize how much we have in common; they would begin to question the puppet masters.

The aristocracy in our country has too much at stake to allow that to happen, so they will continue to pull the strings and control the puppets. It won't last forever, though. The strings are beginning to fray; the children are beginning to question the status quo. They are out in the streets protesting and at home asking questions of their parents, challenging these beliefs that have no grounds, no truths, and no foundation.

Little by little the foundation is crumbling, and the American aristocracy is becoming frantic; they are lying, cheating, and using every means at hand to keep people who don't agree with them from voting or having a say in our democracy.

"No matter how hard you try you can't stop me now."
—**Message from a Black man, The Temptations**

.

Chapter 38

BLACK IS?

*"*C*HANGE WILL NOT COME if we wait for some other person or some other time. We are the ones we've been waiting for. We are the change that we seek."*
—Barack Obama

Early on in life, I found that one of the most beneficial things I can do for myself is to keep in good physical condition. With that in mind, three days a week I would faithfully arise early in the morning and walk or ride my bike to one of our local gyms—Pacific Nautilus—and spend the first hour and a half of my day working out. I wasn't trying to build muscle as much as trying to maintain the few I still had. Everyone knew I wouldn't be available during that time, so they didn't expect to be able to reach me. I chose Pacific Nautilus because it was a no-nonsense, no-frills gym—no walls of mirrors or spandex-clad self-admirers, just free weights, serious workout machines, and dedicated people. The type of folks who frequented Pacific Nautilus were there to either get in shape or maintain the level of conditioning they had.

Eugene at the time was—and still is—not the most diverse city as far as race goes. Black folks coming here from the Midwest or South would call it lily-white. Back then, when you saw another Black person, you'd at least acknowledge them, and more than likely start up a conversation with them, if for no other reason than to see how they ended up in a town like Eugene.

I walked into Nautilus one morning and saw a young Black man who was new to the gym and new to town as far as I could tell. After my workout I struck up a conversation with him in the locker room. James was a tall, muscular guy— athletic-looking with a pronounced scar over his left eye, which I assumed was the result of being in the ring or a street fight. In my conversation with him, it came out that he had never been in a fight. When I started spouting the dialect I had always spoken on the streets he stopped me and said, "Sorry, I didn't grow up like that, and I don't really understand half of what you're saying."

This was perplexing. Here was a Black man who did not fit the idea of a Black man that I'd grown up with. It turned out that James had grown up in an upper-middle-class family, had lived in an affluent mixed neighborhood, had gone to an Ivy League school, and had become a prestigious attorney. Most surprising was that he didn't speak the language—you know, the whole Ebonics thing. But he was still Black. Little did I know that later in life I was to raise three kids that pretty much fit the same mold, and they too are still Black!

It turned out the scar over his eye was the result of being hit with a lacrosse stick. Lacrosse—huh? What the hell is Lacrosse? I'd never heard of Black people playing lacrosse. We played football, basketball, and baseball!

James came from a family of well—educated Black people. Everyone in his family had an advanced college degree and were white-collar professionals, so it was only natural for him to follow suit. There was no peer pressure for him to succumb to, no psychological barriers to overcome, and no danger of him getting involved in gang warfare. He didn't grow up talking Black English, so therefore he didn't feel the need to talk it to fit in. Standard or business English was his native language, and with it he was able to navigate the business and professional world effortlessly—and as far as I could tell, he was still Black.

When I get up in the morning and look in the mirror, I'm Black. When I'm brushing my teeth at night—yep, I'm still Black. There are lots of Black people who feel you need to act a certain way, dress a certain way, and talk a certain way to prove your Blackness; and if you don't, you are selling out.

The fact is, "If you are born Black, it doesn't matter whether you are Harvard educated or uneducated; you're still Black. Whether you are a hustler on the street or president of the United States, if you were born Black, I can guarantee that when you die, and I peek in your coffin—you will still be Black."

You don't have to fit into someone else's preconceived notion of what being Black is to maintain your Blackness. Inner-city Black kids are pressured to act a certain way, and if they don't, they are considered sell-outs. Dare to hit the books or talk standard English, and you are talking White. Peer pressure is a bitch to have to overcome when you want to fit in, and so many Black kids buy into this description of what being Black is.

I dream of a day when the paradigm of "Black is" includes hitting the books; talking however you want, whether it's standard English or Black English; and dressing in any manner you wish as long as it's not offensive—without being ostracized for any of it. I dream of a day when it is cause for celebration among all the Black kids in school when a member of their group is valedictorian or gets accepted to the college of their choice.

I have friends with similar backgrounds as mine who are functioning in professional arenas. We get together occasionally, and when we do, we naturally lapse into the inner-city Black dialect as if we need to get that out of the way. Then after several minutes of this we go back to what has become natural to us, which is standard English. It's almost like we must check in and say, "Okay, we can still do that," or "Yes, we are still Black," and then go on with the business at hand.

My grown kids get to skip this step.

When I was running my businesses, it was hilarious when, after weeks of negotiations by phone, I'd finally meet face-to-face with a vendor or client and see the shock on their face when they discovered this was not the person they thought they were dealing with. But by then it was too late, I had them.

I grew up speaking Black English on the streets, even though it wasn't spoken in my home. The Black English dialect many inner-city kids gravitate to is a fully developed language that allows us to communicate effectively. If only mainstream America could understand that they need to change the way they go about conducting business and buy into this dialect to function effectively, we would be fine. But that's not going to happen anytime soon, so what's the answer?

Do we try to pressure everyone else to talk Black, so they fit in with us? Or do we learn the dominant dialect and speak standard English? Or maybe become bilingual? I don't have the answer to this, but I find it interesting that even many of our present-day rappers revert to standard English when being interviewed.

"Black is" needs a new paradigm. A paradigm that, while being respectful of the rich culture inner-city ghetto style has created, must be expanded to be accepting of all of us, no matter how we talk, what books we read, our level of education, or how we choose to dress. In a perfect world, none of these things would matter, but we live in the United States. Whether you assimilate, create your own hybrid, or choose to keep to your own culture is a choice each of us must make. But be aware of the ramifications of your choice and accept them.

While doing research for this book, I read articles that danced around actually coming out and saying that many aspects of our inner-city Black culture, while being cool, tend to deliver a child who is unprepared for successfully functioning in today's mainstream society. Knowing that I'm going to be chastised for saying this, I'm going to say it:

"Some aspects of inner-city Black culture and schools serving predominantly Black neighborhoods tend to deliver a child who is unprepared for functioning in today's mainstream society."

I'm not saying that Black youths are less intelligent, or that Whites are more intelligent. I'm saying that in too many instances, Black children come out of inner-city schools less prepared than their White counterparts who attend suburban or private White schools.

As a race we are still operating at a deficit. To substantiate this, I will have to go back to pre-emancipation in this country, when it was a crime for anyone to teach a slave to read or write. Early access to reading has been shown to be an important ingredient in childhood development and was absent in African American households back then. It wasn't until 1863 on Roanoke Island that the first escaped former slaves were allowed to attend school, a school set aside for coloreds. From that point forward a select few coloreds were exposed to education, but it was not the same education that was afforded their White counterparts. Schools were segregated and unequal.

Most Colored schools were provided tattered and outdated textbooks that were discarded or handed down from White schools. These textbooks were slanted toward White culture and rarely, if ever, mentioned people of African descent in a positive manner.

Coloreds were generally expected to work in vocational jobs, so in the minds of school administrators, college preparation wasn't necessary. There were several Black colleges that sprang up around the country, but attempts for coloreds to attend better-funded traditionally White colleges were thwarted.

Brown v. Board of Education in 1954 gave more access for Blacks but was met with fierce resistance. Several counties in Virginia and other southern states even chose to close all public schools rather than integrate their schools.

George Wallace famously said, "Segregation now, segregation to-morrow, segregation forever," and stood at the door of one of the southern universities to block the entry of two Black students want-ing to attend the school. Much later, after having been crippled and confined to a wheelchair and realizing what it was like to be discrim-inated against, he recanted his stance and begged for forgiveness. Some of the people who suffered at the former governor's orders were able to forgive—but for some the hurt still ran too deep.

In contrast, the first White school in this country was started in 1635, an extension of the access to western education that had been afforded to Whites in England and other European areas for over 1,030 years. That's fourteen hundred years and fifty generations of advantage given to White families over Black ones. The western style of knowledge and reason passed down in White culture has been intrinsic to White families for most of this time. This way of thinking that allows them to function in mainstream America was foreign to early slaves and freed slaves. I'm not saying that the Western way of thinking is better or worse, but it is the framework we are forced to work within in this country.

In addition, and as a result of this deficit, many parents in African American households don't have higher levels of education and therefore aren't able to pass down the English language skills and western paradigms that are intrinsic in most White households. This means that these skills are sometimes deficient in young Black people who are attempting to enter into mainstream colleges or businesses, putting them at a distinct disadvantage when taking SAT tests or dealing with the curriculum in most colleges.

This is a long-winded way of saying that in essence Whites in this country have a 328-year head start over Blacks to education in this country; in reality a whopping 1,400-year overall jumpstart on western education, thought, and reason; and the same 1,400-year head start on assimilation of western concepts of science, mathematics, the English language over relocated Africans and their descendants. That's quite a deficit to have to overcome in such a short historical time.

In view of this, anyone who is paying attention would have to say that Black people in this country have made tremendous strides, overcoming overwhelming obstacles in a comparatively short amount of time. This progress attests to the intelligence and strength of a people who were brought here against their will to a country with rules and concepts that were—and in some ways still are—foreign to them. If you look at the number of Black executives, scientists, politicians, and business owners, you must marvel at the resilience of Black people in the United States.

We've come a long way.

Chapter 39

PROMISE

Eugene, Oregon

E UGENE IS A MIDSIZED Pacific Northwest town that revolves around outdoor recreation, education, and healthcare. Eugene's school system is one of the best in the state, and South Eugene High School is one of the best in the country, having been inducted into the national Blue Ribbon School Program and receiving a silver ranking in U.S. News & World Report's America's Best Schools survey—partly because of the amount of participation from parents, teachers, and the community. The relative affluence and level of education of Eugene's population does play a role, too, no doubt.

Of the 175,000 souls who reside in Eugene and surrounding area, only 1.4 percent are African Americans—so naturally we tend to gravitate to each other in an unspoken gesture of solidarity.

When our children were young, we had a group of mixed-race and Black folks we hung out with. We'd get together on weekends at the park and let our kids run until they were exhausted. Then on weekdays we would merge back into the White world that Eugene is. Because these kids grew up in this environment, none of them had any major issues with race; however, we did look forward to the weekends and our get-togethers.

I do remember an incident that brought this to light. When Taj was in elementary school, I helped coach his soccer team. Most of our time was spent just trying to get this mob of energetic six-year-old boys to line up in their positions on the field. One spring game, we were playing a team known to be particularly aggressive. The game was going well for us. During a break in play, I looked across the field to see Taj chasing one of the kids from the other team. Taj was not an aggressive kid; he was more into making peace with people, even at that early age. I ran across the field, caught him, and brought him back to the sideline. I asked, "Hey, man, what's going on? Why were you chasing that kid?"

Taj looked at me and said, "He called me a name!"

Of course, my mind jumped to something racial, and I said, "Did he call you a nigger?"

Taj looked at me quizzically and said, "What's a nigger?"

I thought for a moment and finally said, "Never mind, man. You don't need to know right now; you'll learn soon enough. Just go out there and have fun."

All these kids are grown now. Some stayed here in Eugene, and some moved to other parts of the country, but we keep in touch with them and their parents. I recently took stock of these Black and mixed-race kids who grew up together here in Eugene and where they are now in their lives. My children, their friends, and the neighborhood minority kids are good examples of how much your environment can affect your outcome.

Here's a sample of what these kids have accomplished at the time of this writing:

- Taj T.— Bachelor of science degree, University of Oregon. Senior manager, product and marketing analytics at Providence Health and Services

- Jazmin T.—Master's degree in social work (MSW); therapist and Spanish/English interpreter at Strong Integrated Behavioral Health in Eugene, Oregon

- Jonathan B.—director at Portland Parks and Nature Department

- Deva K.—Senior Vice President talent relations and events representative at Showtime Networks in Los Angeles, California

- Jesse R.—assistant director of sales and marketing at BGI Inc.

- David B.—attorney, director of legal operations at NBC Universal; chair of the board of directors at Drama Club NYC

- Micah K.T.—producer, director, associate director on *Dancing With the Stars*, *Expedition Unknown*, *Finding*

Bigfoot, and *Cabin Fever* on National Geographic

- Joseph B.—High school principal

- Daniel B.—technical solutions engineer in Portland, Oregon

- Seth R.—MBA; partner and CMO at Revolutions Design Group in Eugene, Oregon

- Aisha G.—MPH and a PMP; project manager at Center for Outcomes Research and Education

- Nigel, — Software engineer

Most of them have college degrees, they all have successful careers, most of them are helping to create jobs for others, and they're all making substantial contributions to society.

What's different about how these kids were raised? For one thing, they didn't have the five hundred-pound weight called racism to don every day. Although Eugene is one of the whitest cities in the country, and there are certainly instances of racism here, it is not something that smacks you in the face every day when you walk out the door like in some areas of the country. That is a huge burden these kids did not have to deal with. When sixty percent of your mind, body, and soul is occupied with dealing with racism, you can't possibly be operating at one hundred percent.

For another thing, they were able to attend the superb school system that Eugene has. This includes schools where teachers did not spend most of their time dealing with discipline issues that should have been dealt with at home, schools that were well-funded because of property values and the related taxes—and additional private funding. Also, there were no Black neighborhoods or White neighborhoods, and consequently no Black schools or White schools—only good schools. There were no gangs trying to enlist our kids and no pressure to conform to someone else's ideal of what Black is.

The parents of these kids were active in the schools. If there was a problem, we dealt with it. We helped in the classrooms, and we participated in school activities.

Now imagine a nation where all children, no matter what their race, location, or economic class, had this same support and access to quality education.

If we are somehow able to convince the powers-that-be that educating young minorities is not a threat to their hold on power, but will instead benefit their communities, their bank accounts, and the country as a whole, that's when we will begin to see more progress in this country.

The United States spends an average of $45,771 per year to incarcerate a prisoner, but only $17,013 per year to educate a child (2022 dollars). There are currently 1.9 million people residing in prisons. We spend $80.7 million on public prisons and $3.9 million on private prisons per year. Doesn't it make sense to put money into taking measures to prevent these same people from becoming criminals? Consider the adage "An ounce of prevention is worth a pound of cure." This is a tired and worn out saying, but it still holds true.

Every time you stop a school, you will have to build a jail. What you gain at one end you lose at the other. It's like feeding a dog on his own tail. It won't fatten the dog.—**Mark Twain, speech, November 23, 1900**

He who opens a school door closes a prison.
—**Victor Hugo**

As of 2016 the United States, while being the wealthiest nation on Earth, ranked thirty-eighth in math, twenty-fourth in science, and seventh in teacher pay. In overall education, we dropped from sixth place in 1990 to twenty-seventh in 2018; that's a twenty-one-place drop in a truly short time. Of course, there are many factors that go into these statistics that I won't go into here, but still, that's an alarming trend.

I see schoolteachers having to buy their own school supplies for their classes while having to beg to be paid a wage that will keep them in the profession. According to Zip Recruiter 2023 entry-level pay for teachers averages $24,000 to $50,000 per year, which is lower than a carpenter; $29,000 - $69,651 or plumbers; $28,000 - $66,000. Also, while seventy-seven percent of teachers in the USA are female, most don't even get maternity leave—I find that astounding! These are the people in charge of shaping the future of our country; don't you think they should be paid accordingly? Doesn't it make sense that educators should be one of the highest-paid professions in the country?

According to *Education Week*, forty-four percent of teachers leave the profession within the first five years. Many of them leave because the pay scale is not enough to pay their student debt. They must move on to another occupation to be able to live comfortably.

But it's not just about the school systems. We can't send kids off to school and expect teachers to have the responsibility of raising our children. Families and neighborhoods must take responsibility also—that's where it starts. We must somehow change some elements of inner-city Black culture from despair to promise. It starts at the family level when children are infants, and it continues through elementary, middle, and high school. It starts in the home and continues on the streets. It's hard to excel when you are just trying to survive. We must find ways to keep our Black youth from fighting and killing each other—we have to change what so much of our Black culture is. Many of the rappers and other Black artists have realized this and instead of rapping about "shooting niggas and mistreating ho's," they have begun talking about more positive things.

This includes rappers like **2 Chainz** who said;

"I encourage everyone to pay attention to the issues that matter to you, from jobs and the economy to education and our schools, to criminal justice reform. Whatever it is that you care about, make sure you use your voice."

Or as **Beyoncé** said;

"If you feel insignificant, you better think again. Better wake up because you're part of something way bigger.

Or **Chance the Rapper**;

"Something I try to instill in others is to just be a good person. It's a decision you make a million times a day. But if you keep trying, good stuff comes to you in an ordained way."

That's what I'm talking about.

I'm one of the lucky ones. I'm fortunate enough to have been raised in a home environment that valued education and taking responsibility for one's actions, and I had mentors along the way who planted those important seeds. It took a long time for those seeds to sprout, and I took a long, circuitous route to get to where I am today. I happened to be in the right place at the right time, and I met the right people—all these things have added up to get me to this good place that I find myself in now. I'm eternally grateful for that.

There are many more young black and minority youths—promising diamonds in the rough, ready to rise to another level and make positive contributions to our society if given the chance. Let's not let them down, we all stand to gain by giving them the opportunity to reach their promise and we all stand to lose if we don't.

We've come a long way, but we still have a long way to go.

AUTHOR BIOGRAPHY

R ON TINSLEY WAS BORN in Cincinnati, Ohio, in 1947, in a time when Jim Crow laws were still being enforced in many parts of the country. In 1966 he joined the U.S. Army, did training in Fort Knox, Kentucky, and Fort Gordon, Georgia, and then moved on to his permanent duty station in Oahu, Hawaii. There he was introduced to a lifestyle unlike that which he grew up in. After an attempt to relocate back to Cincinnati after his discharge, he realized he was no longer willing to adjust to the inner-city lifestyle and moved back to Hawaii. There Ron enjoyed a successful career as a jazz and R&B vocalist, opening for such artists as the Four Tops, Buddy Miles, and Lou Rawls, and performing on stage with Stevie Wonder, Bonnie Raitt, and Boz Scaggs.

In 1980 Ron moved to Oregon, to fulfill his lifelong dream of being a forest ranger. He worked for the U.S. Forest Service on a wildland firefighting crew and in other areas of forestry.

In 1991, after attending the University of Oregon and obtaining a business degree, he founded Custom Craftworks, a compa-

ny specializing in the manufacture of massage and physical thera-
py equipment. He grew the company from a single-car garage to
the third-largest company in the industry. He also founded Valley
Technology, a company specializing in Anesthesiology and medical
equipment. He also holds numerous patents, including those for the
Epidural Positioning Device, which is used in labor and delivery and
operating rooms worldwide, and for the Cervical Relief Pillow.

Ron now resides in the Pacific Northwest and spends his time
exploring the spectacular rivers and mountains of the Pacific Northwest through backpacking, fly fishing, and floating on the crystal-clear rivers. More than anything, he loves spending time with his
close-knit family.

Made in the USA
Monee, IL
08 October 2023